7 Ways a Baby

Will Change YOUR Life

Bettie B. Youngs, Ph.D., Ed.D.

Susan M. Heim

Jennifer L. Youngs

B/B

burres books

Burres Books an Imprint of Bettie Youngs Book Publishers, www. BettieYoungsBooks.com

If you are unable to order this book from your local bookseller, or online from *Amazon* or *Barnes & Noble* or from the *Espresso Book Machine*, or *Read How You Want*, or from wholesaler *Baker & Taylor*, you may order directly from the publisher: sales@BettieYoungs-Books.com.

Library of Congress Catalog Number 2014914078

eBook ISBN: 978-1-940784-36-6
Trade Paper ISBN: 978-1-940784-37-3

1. Susan M. Heim. 2. Bettie Youngs Books. 3. Problem Solving. 4. Bettie B. Youngs. 5. Children. 6. Family. 7. Self-Esteem. 8. Happiness. 9. Problem Resolution. 10. Parent Education. 11. Self-Image. 12. Jennifer L. Youngs. 13. Kendahl B. Youngs. 14. Bullying. 15. Childhood Behavior.

What People Are Saying About This Book . . .

"Being a parent is a powerful experience, but often we don't anticipate the many ways it will change us. Expectant and new parents will find this book helpful because it examines the very real effects children exert on a parent's sense of 'self,' concept of love, and personal and work goals, and it explores the basis of the deep satisfaction we derive from being a parent. It's the 'what to expect' manual that's real and honest . . . and helpful and hopeful."—**Michael Popkin, Ph.D., author of** *52 Weeks of Active Parenting*

"As a father of nineteen children, senior vice president of the Orlando Magic, a motivational speaker and an author, I know all about balancing the needs of a family with all the other demands of a busy life. The authors perfectly capture the juggling act that parents struggle to perform when a child is added to the family. The challenges of childrearing are great, but the rewards are even greater. Whether you're having your first baby or your fifth, this book is chock-full of wisdom on how to maximize the parenting experience. I highly recommend Oh, Baby!"—**Pat Williams, Senior Vice President of the NBA's Orlando Magic and author of** *How to Be Like Coach Wooden*

"This beautiful book will help parents of young children grow in appreciation for the diligence of heart and plain old hands-on work required in doing the most important job in the world—raising God's children."—**Donna Schuller, Crystal Cathedral Women's Ministries, and co-author,** *Woman to Woman Wisdom: Inspiration for Real Life* **and author of** *Healthy Family, Happy Life*

"You don't just 'add a child' to the family. Parenting is more than the work of caring for an infant, and so much more than showing the little newcomer that he or she is thoroughly loved. A baby's first year does a complete makeover on the new mom and dad—but it also completely transforms the family as a whole. You'll find this book incredibly satisfying to your heart, head and soul."—**Carrie Wilkins, mom to a one-year-old**

"Of all the experiences in a lifetime, raising our children remains one of life's greatest joys and a source of deep satisfaction. This was true for us in raising our four children, and we see this same joy and feeling of contentment in our own children who are now parents. Aside from the really helpful advice that is sure to be of great benefit to parents, this book will help us all internalize the many ways that caring for a baby is a blessing."—**Millard and Linda Fuller, founders,** *Habitat for Humanity* **and** *The Fuller Center for Housing*

"As I write this, the phone is ringing, the baby is screaming at the top of her lungs, and my husband is yelling at me to quiet the baby so he can answer the phone. These new 'post-baby dynamics' are not exactly what I expected!"—**Dede Beckman, new parent**

"Now that I have a one-year-old, I find I have much more in common with others who are parents—and less in common with those who do not. At first I thought, well, this is probably because other parents will let you gush ad nauseam about your cute kid and your 'war stories,' but after reading this book I better understand why becoming a parent is automatic induction into the 'Parents' Club,' which I daresay is very exclusive because its members know things that those without kids simply do not. This book looks at the real truths—the 'secrets'— that make being a parent the epitome of life experiences!"—**Vanessa Geva, Filmore Middle School educator**

"I'm a 'new dad,' and I really love my new status! A baby definitely puts me in the ranks of being a 'grown up,' and it seems like my friends and the people I work with even treat me with more respect! So there are lots of perks to being a dad, but the downsides are loss of independence and the fact that I no longer have my wife all to myself. This book helped me look at these issues through 'new eyes,' to learn how to 'make the trade' without feeling slighted."—**Tom Logan, new dad**

"I made the decision to return to work after the birth of my baby, but I discovered that back to work did not mean 'back to business as usual.' Suddenly, arranging for my morning commute leaves me exhausted before I even get in the car—not to mention that I can't bear to leave my child with a babysitter! This book provides new parents alternatives to 'giving up' and shows them what 'having it all' really means. You'll find this book illuminating. And soul-saving!" —**Rhonda Frohman, new parent**

"Having a baby is a dream come true for many parents, but to really enjoy the fulfillment of that dream takes a realistic approach to the many challenges that new parents face. In this wonderful book, the authors perfectly balance the delights and also the dilemmas of parenthood, and most importantly give you a wealth of solid, practical advice that will help you and your family make the best of both." —**John M. Byrne, author,** *From God-Given to God-Driven: Reclaiming Your Dreams and Fulfilling Your Life*

"Until you 'survive' that first year with your baby, you really can't imagine how having a child changes your life! For me, the first realization hit when I looked around the house for my keys and discovered them in my baby's car seat—along with my wallet, grocery list and a hair tie! The next 'reality check' hit around the eighth month when my husband began calling me 'mom' instead of 'sweetie.' The third was the day I was preparing a 'give-away' bag of clothes that no longer fit my year-old baby, only to find myself placing the bag on a top shelf in the closet and thinking, 'I should keep these to use with my next baby.' That's when I realized that the ways in which I'd changed were not only about the outward things—managing time, being organized—but I'd grown a parent's heart. Family, not independence, is what I want my life to be about. Reading this book made me 'okay' with that realization."—**Jessica Lee, mom to Devron**

"The biggest change for me when I became a mother, aside from the 24/7 job of responding to my baby's needs, was how to find alone time with my husband. I really missed that, especially since you think having a baby will draw you closer, only to realize you have to schedule time to be close! This book helped me understand the deeper issues at play. Great book!"—**Anita Greene, new parent**

Contents

Introduction

Having a Baby Will Change Your Life!

Dear Reader,

If you've picked up this book or received it as a gift, chances are you're a mother- or father-to-be or the parent or stepparent of a new baby, whether it's your first or your fifth! Congratulations! We are so very happy for you. Or perhaps you're considering having a child—even adding to the family of older kids—and you want to know, "What is it really going to be like to have a new baby?"

Certainly, a child is a miracle—and a bundle of love who will add zest to your life and zeal to your heart. Most people rate having and raising children as one of the most important and rewarding experiences in life. Most people say, "My greatest accomplishment is my children." Indeed, the joys and challenges of child-rearing will have an impact on every day of your life (even when grown!); but that first year of baby's life is particularly special—and challenging. The rewards are many and wonderful, but the reality is this: It's also probably going to be quite different from what you imagined.

Are we ever really prepared for our first child? Or even the second or third? Oh sure, we've got the nursery decorated and stocked and the pediatrician selected, but we're often shocked at how, despite our best efforts, we're totally unprepared for parenthood. Unfortunately, babies don't come with instruction manuals. Most parents tell us, "I never imagined I could love someone as much as I love my child. But I also never anticipated the way this child completely took over my life and changed it in so many ways. It wouldn't have made me change my mind about having a child—definitely no regrets there! But I think I would have had more realistic expectations about parenthood in the first year, and the adjustment wouldn't have been so difficult."

Even parents who already have a child, whom you would expect to be in the know about what it's like in baby's first year, are often unprepared for the realities of dealing with two (or more!) children at once. This new child, with his different needs and personality traits, can certainly throw a monkey wrench into an already established family. Many new parents think a child will fit seamlessly into their marriage and their lives, but the road is often much bumpier than they expected.

Of course, the parenting experience is different for everyone. Not all couples will experience the same stresses to the same degree. But it's been our experience that the seven areas of life described in this book will be affected in some significant way for nearly all parents. That's why this book is so very important. Not only will we clue you in to the challenges and joys you'll experience in the first year of parenthood, but we also intend to help you get through them in the best way possible! For instance, each chapter includes Questions for Discussion that will help you and your parenting partner really think about these issues and, most importantly, communicate in ways that can resolve any conflicts between you and allow you to experience the wonder of your baby together. We'll also provide helpful Action Steps that offer concrete and doable suggestions for tackling each issue. And each chapter includes a story of one family's journey through the first crucial year with a new baby. We're certain that you'll see a lot of similarities between their situations and yours. Finally, you'll read quotes from other parents, both well known and not so well known, reflecting on their experiences of new parenthood. Honest and sometimes humorous, they'll provide little nuggets for you to think about on those days when you're wondering if you'll make it through!

We're so excited to be going on this journey with you. As parents ourselves, we've been where you are now. In fact, we daresay that our lives, relationships, and careers today are the direct result of the amazing experiences we've shared in being parents. Since we gave birth to our little "newcomers," our lives haven't been the same, and yours will change too. As you overcome the challenges and savor the rewards, you'll find yourself more fulfilled than you ever imagined.

—the Authors

One

*A Baby Will Open
Your Heart . . . Like
No Other Love Can
or Ever Will*

> Most people think they know what it's like to have love in their lives—until they have a child. Then they realize that they never had this kind of love!

What is the first word that comes to mind when you think of having a child? Most likely, it's "love." What greater love exists on this earth than that of a parent for a child? Love is what keeps us going when times are tough. Love gives us hope and strength. It brings joy to our lives, but it also exposes us to its bittersweet side: worry and even heartache. But it's worth it. There's no way more guaranteed to bring love into your life, to bring meaning to your existence, than to have a child. It will transform your definition of love. Oftentimes, we don't understand what real love is until we have a child. Then we know. It is all-encompassing, consuming, unconditional, and life-changing. And you will be blessed by it.

When Marla and Brian met, they both knew it was love at first sight. They worked for the same large company, but Brian was in the international division while Marla worked in the public relations department of the domestic division. If it hadn't been for the winter ice storm that knocked out electricity in part of the city one day, they might never have met. The company had nearly 600 employees housed in two large buildings, each served by its own parking lot. Brian worked in one building and Marla worked in the other. But on that day, with the elevators not functioning, they all had to use the stairs of their respective buildings, which emptied into the same area on the street.

> *Love is wanting to have children together because they are the exclamation point of love.*
>
> —Liz Carpenter

The moment Marla saw Brian, she thought, "Wow, what a beautiful man!" Immediately, she checked to see if he wore a wedding band; he noticed and confirmed, "Not married!" Then he added with a great smile, " . . . and not dating anyone, either. Unless you're free for dinner . . . "

To make a long story short, they spent the next year cooking together, shopping for wine, entertaining friends, checking out cozy restaurants, going to the theater, and strategizing about how each of them could move up the ladder in their respective jobs at the company. They looked for every possible opportunity to be in each other's company. If one was heading to a certain restaurant for a business lunch, the other managed to have lunch at that restaurant, too—pretending, of course, not to know each other. It was fun! They liked each other's friends. They toasted each other's successes and held each other through the down times. And when they reached the point where parting at the end of a date was simply too painful, they got engaged. Six months later, they were married.

The first year of marriage was sweet and passionate, and it passed quickly. When their second anniversary rolled around and they talked about buying a gift to commemorate it, they decided that having a baby would be the most appropriate gift they could give each other. Marla recalls, "Our feelings for each other were so deep. I wanted 'his' child, 'his' children. And even though he had once told his friends that he didn't necessarily see marriage or kids in his future, when we met and fell in love, having a child, children, and a family was a natural progression—an expression of our love for each other." Brian and Marla felt they had already been blessed by the magic of love, but when they confirmed that Marla was expecting, they knew yet another, and even deeper, shade of love.

Samantha Rae arrived almost seven weeks premature and spent the first three weeks in an incubator. Marla and Brian went to the hospital on a daily basis. They were so worried. The baby was so tiny and fragile . . . a little being clinging to life. Their hearts went out to her. They felt completely helpless. They cried a lot together . . . especially as they left the hospital after seeing their daughter. They were amazed that they already loved her so deeply! But their hearts were also pained. They loved their little girl more than words could describe.

Marla had planned to take a three-month maternity leave and then return to work, but when she was told that Samantha would not be going home for at least three to five weeks, Marla returned to work, thinking it was the only way to help the time go by. Since the hospital was downtown and just a few blocks from her office building, it seemed like the best way to be near Samantha, especially since she and Brian could slip out of work and visit her when they wanted to.

Nearly two months after the birth, they finally took Samantha home. At that point, Marla made the decision not to return to work. Their baby's health was still too fragile, and they just couldn't consider leaving her in the care of anyone else.

Today, Samantha is three years old and a healthy and happy little girl. Brian says, "Samantha has opened us up to so many new ways to share in our love for her. It's a different life, I'll say that! In the first year and a half, we worried a lot. We even had to rush her to the hospital a couple of times after we brought her home—we were frightened to death. But the last year and a half has brought us mostly laughter and fun. Our daughter has enriched our lives so much."

> *Love is what you've been through with somebody.*
>
> —James Thurber

Marla adds, "We just love our little daughter so much, and it's a love that is greater—and different—than anything I can describe. I

3

love my husband, and he loves me. But we love our baby more than we can put into words. I'd have to say that having a child is a definition of love all its own. For us, our baby—a 'gift' to each other, one grown out of our own love for each other—has produced a kind of love, a depth of love, that is simply in a league of its own. Samantha's arrival has also strengthened and sweetened our relationship with our parents; it's gone a long way toward healing Brian's relationship with his father. And it's introduced us to other parents, many of whom have become dear friends. This baby has so expanded the love we get and give to others. It's amazing, and it's a blessing in our lives. Just as Liz Carpenter said, children are the 'exclamation point of love'! How very true this has been for Brian and me."

> *Making the decision to have a child—it's momentous. It is to decide forever to have your heart go walking around outside your body.*
>
> —Elizabeth Stone

FOUR WAYS A BABY WILL INTRODUCE YOU TO THE PERILS OF LOVE

Most people think they know what it's like to have love in their lives—until they have a child. Then they realize that they never had this kind of love! Your love for your child is unique, and distinct from any other love you'll ever experience. It is a wonderful love, but also a painful one. It's the best feeling in the world, but it will bring up so many other emotions as well. Marla and Brian found out what love really meant when Samantha was born.

You'll Learn the Meaning of Sacrificial Love

Sacrifice involves loss. When you have a child, you willingly give up anything to protect her, keep her safe, fulfill her needs, and ensure her happiness. You may leave the big city you love because you feel she'll be safer in the country. Or you may leave the country to be closer to family and schools, or to have quicker and better access to medical facilities. You're willing to give up the career you've pursued for years because it takes you away from the child you love. Or you may find a new job because the added expenses of bringing up a child require that you earn more income. You'll even give up a dream—running for office, climbing a mountain—if there's a possibility that it could lead to harm for your child. Or you may decide to do these things now because you are inspired and motivated to excel at what once scared you, or that you had no interest in doing. Or now that you're a parent, you may wish to pave the way and make the world a better, safer place for all children. And there's a good chance that you'll find great joy and contentment in watching your child accomplish her dreams instead of focusing solely on your own. You take pride in her achievements and realize that being the "wind beneath her wings" becomes your greatest source of satisfaction. Your own life holds less value for you now in comparison to hers. You learn the true meaning of sacrifice—and you're willing to make it. How splendid the effect our children have on us!

> *When the satisfaction or the security of another person becomes as significant to one as one's own satisfaction or security, then the state of love exists.*
> —Henry Stack Sullivan

Marla once dreamed of advancing in her career, but when Samantha was born with health problems, she didn't think twice about who needed her most. While she rued the loss of all the progress she'd made advancing in her field, the mother's love she felt for her baby demanded no less than caring for her in these important first years of life. As Marla said, "If I had it to do all over again, I'd make the same decision. It was a sacrifice I was willing to make because of my love for Samantha."

Questions for Discussion

❀ What sacrifices have you made in your life to be a parent?

_____

_____

❀ Do you regret giving up any of the dreams or plans you've had?

_____

_____

✿ If you had it to do all over again, would you make the same decisions?

_____

_____

✿ Do you think that women and men share equally in the sacrifices they make for their children? Why or why not?

_____

_____

> ## Take Action!
>
> Think about a sacrifice you've made for the sake of your child. Now make two columns on a piece of paper: one for listing what you've lost and the other for listing what you've gained. Do this for anything you've had to put aside or give up because you became a parent. Most likely, you'll find that the gains column will be much longer than the losses column. The next time you get a twinge of nostalgia for the career you gave up or the town you left behind, or whatever other sacrifices you might have made, pull out your list and focus on what you've gained. You'll be counting your blessings in no time.

Although Marla had to give up a job she loved, she stayed in touch with her closest coworkers and kept up her contacts in case she might be able to return to her career in the future. After Samantha's health stabilized and she was "out of the woods," Marla was also able to freelance from her home for one or two small clients. She was making much less money than before, but it helped keep her public

> *I have found the paradox that if I love until it hurts, then there is no hurt, but only more love.*
>
> —Mother Teresa

relations skills fresh and allowed her to keep a foot in the door of a field she loves and may someday return to.

You'll Shoulder Enormous Responsibility

Raising a child is a major responsibility. Who among us does not soon find that children need enormous amounts of our time and energy—not to mention that in the first year they bind us to the house and restrict our once-carefree lives? Children keep us up throughout the night, needing comfort and soothing, especially when they are ill or cutting teeth. And yet, mysteriously, we parents do not find the responsibility of this sort of care-taking burdensome or bothersome. In fact, we find great joy in it! Fifteen minutes after finally rocking your baby back to sleep at 3 A.M., you need only stand at the crib and watch as he lies peacefully asleep, and you'll find a smile in your heart.

A man who becomes conscious of the responsibility he bears toward a human being . . . will never be able to throw away his life. He knows the "why" for his existence, and will be able to bear almost any "how."

—Victor Frankl

Because Samantha was premature, Brian and Marla took on the enormous responsibility of caring for her. They had to administer medications, hook up various monitors and alarms, schedule visits with specialists and therapists, and shoulder the increased worry and fear that accompany the birth of a fragile little being. But out of this huge burden arose a love so fierce that Marla and Brian would do anything they possibly could for their child's welfare. They willingly took on the added responsibility for Samantha's care—because of their love.

Questions for Discussion

❀ What added responsibilities have you taken on with the birth of your child?

_____

_____

❀ Do you think you're a more responsible person now that

you're a parent? In what ways?

_____

_____

❀ Do you feel the burden of your increased responsibilities, but willingly shoulder them?

_____

_____

❀ How have your increased responsibilities added to the love that you feel for your child?

_____

_____

> ## Take Action!
>
> If your responsibilities sometimes feel overwhelming, don't shoulder them all alone. This is especially true if your child has special needs. Don't be afraid to ask for help. If your partner is already as consumed by work as you are, ask family members or friends to give you a breather. Don't feel that you have to "do it all." It's not a sign of weakness to accept others' assistance. In fact, it's a very wise thing to do because it will keep you healthy and sane enough to give your baby the best possible care!

Marla and Brian were fortunate to have family members close by, and were very grateful for the assistance! Both sets of grandparents often came over to help lighten the load. Marla's sister, a nurse, often came by to check Samantha over, and reassured them that they didn't have to worry or be needlessly fearful. It was a big relief to Brian and Marla not to have to shoulder the responsibility for their baby's care alone.

Your Child's Welfare Will Always Lie Heavy on Your Heart

Your great love for your child means you'll never be worry-free again. Every car crash or crime you hear about will make you think, "Was my child involved?" or "What if that had happened to us?" When your child hurts, you hurt. If another child picks on yours, you'll have to restrain yourself from demanding that this kid give your child more respect! You'll want to protect your child like a mother bear protects her helpless little cub from predators. And suddenly, the world seems like a very dangerous place. Anytime you read about the death of a child, it brings home the fact that your child is never entirely safe—and that parents can't completely protect them from everything. Even when a child is grown, the worries never go away. Will my "baby" find a job after college? Is my daughter's husband good to her? Will my son have to go to war? Your child's welfare will always be on your mind, and lie heavily on your heart.

> *One thing I know is that when [my daughter] starts driving, I'm not going to get any sleep. I'm already planning it all out, you know? Can I put cameras in the car? Can I put in a tracking device? I'm already totally obsessing about it—and she's not even two!*
>
> —Leah Remini

Marla and Brian got a head start on their worrying when Samantha was born prematurely. Not only did they have the normal concerns that new parents have, but they had to deal with the complications that can arise when a baby enters the world too soon. Even though Samantha is now considered to be in excellent health, they still worry. "Samantha's already been through so much," they say. "What if more problems arise in the future? Can we handle them?" Marla was the first to admit that her hand always seemed to be poised over the phone during the first few years. She was ready to call the doctor every time Samantha had a coughing spell! Brian babyproofed every possible item in the house to keep Samantha safe. And there is no doubt in their minds that when Samantha starts dating, every potential suitor will have to endure a very rigorous screening process! Brian says, "I intend to interview each one before I let her out of the house!"

Questions for Discussion

❀ Does your love for your child increase your worries?

9

_____

_____

❀ Do the dangers in the world concern you a lot more now that you're a parent?

_____

_____

❀ Do you think you'll worry less, more, or about the same as your child gets older? Why?

_____

_____

Take Action!

Although you can't completely stop yourself from worrying, it's wise not to let your concerns overwhelm your child. Sheltering a child from all new experiences could have negative consequences, such as making him overly fearful and timid, or causing him to rebel against your protection in later years. Sure, your heart is going to be in your throat the first time your son takes a ski trip with friends, but he needs to test his wings just as you did at his age. Of course, reasonable precautions should always be taken. For example, make sure that you are well acquainted with the parents in a household where your child will be staying. And always insist that your child wear protective equipment when engaging in sports. Do what you can to keep your child safe, but then let go. Share your worries with other parents—they're guaranteed to understand your plight!

The first time Samantha had a babysitter other than family members, Brian and Marla were a nervous wreck. When Samantha started crying as they headed out the door, they almost ditched their plans and came running back into the house. But they knew that her separation anxiety was the sign of a healthy little girl, so they wiped the tears from their own eyes and hurried out to the car. Of course, they called three times from the restaurant that night, but when they heard that Samantha quit crying about five minutes after they left and was contentedly watching a Barney video, they were relieved. When they got home, they found she had gone to bed without a peep. Marla and Brian vowed to continue with their dates despite the pain they always felt at leaving Samantha. They trusted that she was in capable hands, and knew that it was good for her to learn to feel the comforting arms of another, and to socialize with others. And it was beneficial for their marriage to spend time alone together!

> _The mother-child relationship is paradoxical and, in a sense, tragic. It requires the most intense love on the mother's side, yet this very love must help the child grow away from the mother, and to become fully independent._
> —Erich Fromm

You Can and Will Feel Disappointed at Times

When you know your child is the most wonderful child in the world, you have high expectations for her. Unfortunately, there are going to be times when she will let you down. Perhaps your son is "difficult," always fussing, crying, or screaming, and when you long to show him off at your workplace he lets you down by making a scene. Maybe your daughter doesn't walk until she's fourteen months old (and you have to put up with your sister's bragging that her child walked at ten months!). Perhaps your son's just not all that interested in being around other children, or in being a "good boy" when you're around others. Your heart may grieve when your child's not interested in sports, especially if you were the star quarterback on your school team. You know he could be great, but he just doesn't live up to your expectations of him.

> _If a child lives with acceptance and friendship, he learns to find love in the world._
> —Dorothy Law Nolte

Your children are not always going to see in themselves what you see in them. And they're not always going to give you what you want from them. Although your child will certainly provide you with unconditional love, it's not fair for you to expect her to meet all your emotional needs. If your friend's child just won a "beautiful baby" contest and your kid is content to smear jelly in her hair rather than pose for the camera, you may feel a twinge of impatience that she's not doing what you would like. If your dreams to be a great pianist or writer didn't come to fruition, it's not reasonable to expect your children to have the same dreams so you can enjoy them vicariously. Maybe they will follow your lead . . . but maybe they won't. And putting pressure on your son or daughter to meet your expectations will only lead to anxiety later.

Brian had been on the swimming team throughout college and often led his teammates to victory at swim meets. He even tried out for the Olympic team, but failed to make the cut. So he couldn't wait to get Samantha started in the pleasures of swimming. But the first time her foot touched the pool water, she let out a scream and clung to her mother, refusing to go in even though both Brian and Marla promised to keep her safe. Samantha was absolutely terrified of the water. The more they tried to get her to go in, the more she resisted. The purchase of cute little pool toys seemed to have no effect on her attitude. Samantha looked adorable in her new little bathing suit, but it was destined to stay on dry land along with Samantha. Brian had to admit that he was greatly disappointed, but he knew not to pressure her. She had to learn at her own pace.

> *He who expects much will be often disappointed; yet disappointment seldom cures us of expectation . . .*
>
> —Samuel Johnson

Questions for Discussion

❀ What are your hopes and dreams for your child?

_____

_____

❀ Do you have any unfulfilled dreams for yourself that you hope your child will accomplish?

_____

❀ Has your child ever disappointed you by not meeting your expectations? What if she does this in the future—how will you react?

_____

_____

❀ Do you feel that you met your own parents' expectations of you?

_____

_____

Take Action!

Did you know that Thomas Edison didn't talk until he was four years old? His parents were probably concerned about him, but he never disappointed them. They loved him for himself. When a teacher complained that Tom asked too many questions instead of conforming, his parents decided to homeschool him so he could learn in his own ways. Needless to say, Thomas Edison blossomed because his parents didn't force him to meet certain expectations. They let him move at his own pace and respected his uniqueness. This is a lesson that all parents can learn. No doubt about it, your child will disappoint you at some point in life. Probably more than once! Instead of becoming upset about it, make a list of his unique and wonderful qualities. Focus on what he does well, not on what you want him to do. Never let your child sense your disappointment if he fails to be an athlete or a scholar like you. Praise him for having the courage to be himself.

When Samantha was eventually diagnosed with asthma, Brian knew that he had to give up his dreams of making her into a competitive swimmer. But when Brian and Marla noticed how much Saman-

> *The greatest gift a parent can give a child is unconditional love. As a child wanders and strays, finding his bearings, he needs a sense of absolute love from a parent. There's nothing wrong with tough love, as long as the love is unconditional.*
>
> —President George Herbert Walker Bush

tha loved to use her crayons and do craft projects, they enrolled her in an art class. Samantha loved it with all her heart, and her teacher said she showed "great promise," even at her young age. Whether or not she becomes a well-known artist, Marla and Brian are pleased to encourage her interests and give her every opportunity to pursue her own dreams.

FIVE WAYS A BABY WILL BRING MORE LOVE INTO YOUR LIFE

But if love were accompanied only by sacrifice, responsibility, worry, and disappointment, no one would seek it. There must be so much more to this feeling of love! And indeed there is. That's why we hunger to bring love into our lives through the birth of a child—the rewards of love far outweigh the perils.

You'll Receive Unconditional Love

Love without conditions is a rarity. God loves you unconditionally. Hopefully your parents do. Your spouse . . . well, you're not always convinced that you merit his or her unconditional love. But the love of a child certainly falls into this category. Have you ever read those heartbreaking stories where children have been verbally or physically abused by their parents . . . but still want nothing more than to live with them? Children are programmed to love their parents. It is a bond like no other. They just love you, no matter what. Certainly, you're by no means perfect. Perhaps you're a terrible cook or a mediocre golfer, and have cellulite on your thighs and no patience for heavy traffic. But none of those things matter to your child. She loves you in spite of your imperfections. Isn't it wonderful?

When Marla quit her job, she felt the loss of being praised for something at which she excelled. She'd been popular at work because she was good at what she did and had great public relations instincts. Now that she spent her days at home, she didn't feel particularly skilled at anything. Her cookies crumbled, her clothes came out of the dryer wrinkled, and she gave up trying to reupholster her dining room chairs after she just couldn't get the hang of it. But when Samantha gobbled up her crumbling cookies and pronounced them "the bestest!" Marla no longer cared that they weren't perfect. And when Samantha adopted an old faded beanbag as her favorite chair, it became Marla's best piece of furniture, too. Samantha didn't care if Marla wasn't a great cook, laundress, or decorator. To her, she was just the best mom, and that was enough.

> *To a child's ear, "mother" is magic in any language.*
>
> —Arlene Benedict

Questions for Discussion

🌸 Do you believe in unconditional love? Why or why not?

_____

_____

🌸 Do you feel more loved now that you're a parent?

_____

_____

🌸 In what ways does your child show you that she loves you?

_____

_____

🌸 Has your child brought more love into your life? In what ways?

_____

_____

> **Take Action!**
> The next time you're feeling sorry for yourself, treat yourself to a dose of "baby love!" After an afternoon of fighting rude people at the supermarket or dealing with an unrepentant customer service representative, head over to your child for a loving hug. Hold her close and just breathe in that wonderful baby smell. Remind yourself that she loves you as much as you love her—and that all is right with the world.

You'll Become a More Compassionate and Loving Person

A baby who has bonded with his parents learns to need them, to want them, to love them. To feel this love, to be loved so completely, teaches you the "feel" of love. Feeling loved can open your heart to caring deeply about the well-being of others and to feeling compassionate toward them. In wanting to do all you can to ensure the protection of the helpless little being in your own household, you'll find yourself aching for others who don't have the same protection. Pictures of impoverished children will remind you that it could have been your child's fate—and you'll be more motivated than ever to do something about it. How many parents in the world wish their children weren't being brought up amid poverty or warfare? Your heart bleeds for them and their families, and you fully understand how much other parents must love their children and want the best for them.

To the world you might be one person, but to one person you might be the world.

—Anonymous

After Samantha was born prematurely, Marla wondered how other parents coped. She wanted to provide better support for all parents of premature infants. As she lingered in hospital lounges while Samantha was so sick, she found herself bonding with the other parents who had children in the neonatal intensive care unit. It was such a relief to share her pain with those who could really understand it. After Samantha got better, Marla started a Web site for parents of "preemies." Through this connection, parents could meet others with similar problems and share their concerns and solutions. Marla often went online to advise those who were still going through the pain of having a child in the hospital—not knowing if the baby would live or die—and she rejoiced every single time another baby went home. It was Marla's new mission to help other parents get through the first few difficult months of their babies' lives. It brought great joy to her heart.

> *Perhaps the greatest social service that can be rendered by anybody to this country and to mankind is to bring up a family.*
> —George Bernard Shaw

Questions for Discussion

❀ When you read about children growing up in impoverished conditions, do you wish you could save them all? Has this feeling intensified since you became a parent?

_____

_____

❀ Are you a more compassionate person now?

_____

_____

❀ What can you do today to take the first step in acting compassionately toward others?

_____

_____

> ### Take Action!
> Unfortunately, we can't save the world. But we can do our part. Talk to your spouse about causes that are really important to you. Oftentimes, we become involved because of something that affects our families or friends, such as a cancer diagnosis or a job loss. Talk about how your family can contribute to a worthy cause, whether with time, money, or prayers. If your child were in trouble, wouldn't you want others to reach out to you? Let others know you care.

Your Love for Your Partner Will Grow

You and your spouse now share something that no two other people will ever share—your child. And you both love your child with all your hearts. By witnessing the love your partner has for your baby, you'll grow to love him or her even more. You will love the way he or she plays with your child or changes his diapers—for reasons you would have found totally unromantic before you had the baby. Whereas before it was "He has a cute butt!" or "He dresses nicely," now it's "He doesn't freak out over spit-up on his tie" and "He always makes sure we have formula in the house." Now that's sexy! The love and tenderness that a parent shows for a child are unbelievably appealing. What man hasn't melted at the sight of the mother of his baby lulling her to sleep in a rocking chair? It is total gratitude and love for the life you created together.

> *What matters? It's children. It's human being. It's love. It's making a difference in somebody's life.*
>
> —Celine Dion

Brian never thought he could love his wife more than he had when they got married—until they had Samantha. When he saw how she gave up her formerly slim body for the sake of carrying their child; when he witnessed the sacrifices she made to be at Samantha's side;

when he saw the patience she exhibited when Samantha was ill, he loved Marla more than ever. He marveled at what a beautiful person she was on the inside, even more beautiful than the outside that he had first adored. He felt truly fortunate that she had chosen him to be the father of her child.

Questions for Discussion

❀ Has having a child together increased your love for your spouse?

_____

_____

_____

But if I didn't love [my husband] before I had my baby, I definitely love him now. I have a man who comes home from work at four o'clock after opening his diner at six in the morning and his daughter is literally put in his arms. He doesn't even have a minute to shower or go to the bathroom and he never says, "I just walked in the door." Never.

—Leah Remini

❀ What do you love most about your partner? Have you added to this list since you became parents?

_____

_____

❀ Do you think that being a loving parent makes a person sexy?

_____

_____

> ### Take Action!
>
> The next time your spouse irritates you by throwing his clothes on the floor or forgetting to pick up milk on the way home, hold a picture of your partner with your child in your mind. Think about how she lovingly tucks your baby into bed at night. Consider how enormous his hands look on your baby's tiny little back. Think about being a family. Know that being together and loving each other are far more important than the minor infractions we're all guilty of. Love your partner for who he or she is: your baby's parent. Remember, you chose each other for a reason.

You'll Share a Common Bond with Other Parents

At no time will you feel more a part of the "sisterhood of women" or the "brotherhood of men" than when you become a parent. If you're a new mother, you suddenly feel a connection with other women of the earth. You cherish your special place in the world as the bearer of new life. You feel a bond with women who have tried to make the world safer for your child by working to end world hunger, war, or drunken driving. You feel proud to be a woman. Men, too, experience a new kinship with fellow daddies. You bond together at ball games with your children, camping trips with your little Scouts, and touch football games at the local park.

Marla had to admit that when she was an executive, she looked down a bit on those women who stayed home with their children. She thought that they had chosen the easy way out by opting not to "work" and instead "play" with their children all day. Her perspective changed completely when she became a stay-at-home mom to her daughter. She developed a new appreciation for women who spent their days raising a child. It certainly wasn't the cushy job that Marla had imagined! In fact, she was more exhausted at the end of the day now than she had been after eight hours at the office! Most of all, she knew the absolute importance of the job of motherhood. Mothers, she realized, were so essential to the raising of a precious human being, a capable and self-confident kid, and a wonderful world citizen. Marla now had a renewed respect for all mothers—both stay-at-home and working ones—as they all were doing their best to accomplish the most crucial purpose in life: to nurture a child.

Questions for Discussion

❀ Do you see the job of parenthood as being just as important as other jobs?

_____

_____

❀ Has this perspective forged a greater bond between you and other parents?

_____

_____

❀ Do you have a new respect for parents now that you are one?

_____

_____

❀ How do you feel about being a man or a woman now that you've created a child? Are you proud to be part of the motherhood or fatherhood "club?"

_____

_____

❀ In what ways are you proud?

_____

_____

> ## Take Action!
>
> If you're a woman, make a list of reasons why you love being a woman and a mother. (Examples: "I get to wear pink without looking silly!" "I get to feel the joy of a baby moving within me." "I can get gray hair and wrinkles, but my child still loves me!") If you're a man, list the reasons why you love being a man and a father. (Examples: "I can get away with still acting like a kid." "Fewer undergarments!") Now switch lists with your spouse and laugh together! You might even think of some things to add to each other's list! You'll have fun comparing the joys of being a man or a woman.

You'll Love the Little Things in Life

If you were always hurrying through life before, being a parent forces you to slow down, literally and figuratively! When it takes half an hour to walk to the park because your little one keeps stopping to examine every rock and bug along the way, you'll learn the meaning of patience, for sure. But you'll also gain a new appreciation for the little things in life. Just hearing your child laugh at a silly story or ooh and ahh over bubbles floating through the air will make you appreciate these simple pleasures. When your little one gets all excited over the train whizzing by, you'll see it not as an inconvenience that forces you to stop, but as a wonderful new sight and sound for your growing child. You'll be amazed at how excited you'll suddenly feel about M&Ms, dandelions, and worms; your child will introduce you to a whole new world of wonder! When you look back on your son's or daughter's childhood some day, you won't remember the fancy clothes they had or the expensive car seat you bought. You'll remember the sweet poem he wrote on your Valentine or the time she

> *Being a full-time mother is one of the highest salaried jobs in my field since the payment is pure love.*
>
> —Mildred B.
> Vermont

wanted to save the life of the spider in her room. These are the things that will matter most to you, as Brian and Marla found.

Marla and Brian used to plan how to climb the corporate ladder; now they planned the best spots for a picnic. Whereas they used to look for restaurants that were ideal for entertaining a client, they now sought out those that had highchairs and children's menus. While they used to look forward to socializing with coworkers, now they were just as happy playing outside with Samantha. It was life's simple pleasures that now enthralled them. Although Marla used to love the beautiful roses that Brian sent on her birthday, she loved even more the wild daisies that Samantha picked from a nearby field on Mother's Day. Homemade presents and noodle necklaces beat a crystal vase and a diamond bracelet any day!

> *Enjoy the little things, for one day you may look back and realize they were the big things.*
>
> —Robert Brault

Questions for Discussion

❀ Do you find yourself happier now with a simpler life?

_____

_____

❀ What pleasures of life have you rediscovered now that you're a parent?

_____

_____

❀ How has having a child opened up your eyes to the wonders of the world?

_____

_____

❀ What is one of your child's greatest pleasures?

_____

_____

> **Take Action!**
>
> The next time you're tempted to make big plans, think small instead. Trade the crowds of an amusement park for a camping trip at a state park. Forgo the birthday party at "Chucky Ducky's" for bubble-blowing contests in the back yard. Instead of buying an expensive card, make one with your child. Don't buy a fancy cake at the bakery; whip up cupcakes on your own! You'll be teaching your child the value of living life purely and simply. Best of all, you'll have more fun!

CONCLUSION

Parenting is the greatest textbook for Love 101. It will teach you the true meaning of love. It will show you the pleasures of love, as well as its sorrows. It will bring a love into your life that can never be taken away. You'll become an expert in love from the time you hold your firstborn in your arms. Shower your child with love and feel it returned tenfold. Having a child will show you the way. Your life will be blessed.

Two

A Child . . . Helps You Develop a Durable, Reliable— and Authentic—Sense of Self

Feeling complete is a wonderful sensation, no doubt about it! And nothing contributes to your feeling complete quite like being a parent and helping your little one develop into a happy, loving, and capable person. Helping your child feel safe and emotionally secure is no small feat, and it's hugely important: It is the basis of self-esteem.

Self-esteem is the regard we hold for ourselves. It's a composite picture of self-value, the worth we feel. It's our "total score," our price tag, so to speak. This self-picture is important, in that it colors how willing and able we feel to confront each day's challenges and do our best to the degree we can. It's been said that perhaps nothing affects our health, energy, peace of mind, the goals we set and achieve, the quality of our relationships, or our competence quite so much as the state of our self-esteem. For example, the higher your self-esteem, the more resilient you are to problems and defeats. In the face of adversity, a positive sense of self serves as a powerful coping strategy for overcoming obstacles. It helps you compensate for weaknesses and setbacks and acts as a buffer, in that you are less likely to unduly magnify life's challenges or victories. The worth you feel shows in your actions: the responsibility you take for the choices you make. It's pretty important stuff, especially when it comes to parenting and raising our children.

Certainly, your parenting actions in that first year of your baby's life—and every year thereafter, for that matter—are determining factors in helping your children feel safe, secure, and loving. But it's a two-way street, isn't it? Parents feel better about themselves when they see themselves being good parents; but they need to be pretty secure in themselves first. If parents raise their children with love and affection, help them believe in their abilities and fundamental goodness, allow them to experience consistent and benevolent acceptance, give them the supporting structure of appropriate rules and reasonable expectations, allow them to learn from their mistakes without being shamed, and don't assail them with ridicule, humiliation, or physical abuse as means of controlling them, then children have a good chance internalizing those attitudes and thereby acquiring the foundation for a healthy sense of self. So children have the best chance to grow up feeling safe, secure, wanted, and loved when they have parents who themselves feel safe, secure, wanted, and loved. If parents possess these feelings, model them, and instill them in their children, their children are more likely to have high self-esteem. And a secondary bonus is this: Just as nothing better ensures that our children develop a healthy sense of self than having parents who themselves are whole, nothing contributes to our own positive sense of self than helping our children achieve a durable sense of self for themselves.

We really get a sense of ourselves in our parenting, don't we? If caring for a young child does anything, it lets us see and experience ourselves as willing and capable to meet their needs. Sometimes we measure up; sometimes we want to but we don't. Perhaps of all the many ways we see ourselves over the course of a lifetime, no greater lens exists than that through which we see and judge ourselves as parents. Most parents would agree that parenting is central to the deep satisfaction and pain we experience during our lives. Just listen to senior citizens reminisce and you'll hear them express the same desires. They never wish for a little more time to make more money or express regret at not having acquired more material objects. Rather, they measure life's success by the great joy and satisfaction they experienced in the most precious and valuable moments—those spent with their children. For parents who truly experience this challenging role in a purposeful way, it is the most joyful and rewarding of their lifetime. Parenting is purposeful. Being a child's hero gives meaning to who we are and directs us to be our best. Being a parent is one of the surest ways to become a better you.

Yes, parenting completes us. It's tough for us parents to say that life has little or no meaning or that we have nothing of great worth in our lives. The majority of men and women on earth hope one day to be parents or to help children learn and grow in some way. In fact, people who struggle with infertility often express the sorrow that something is missing from their lives. They'll never feel complete, they say, until they join the "circle of life" and bear children. And indeed, when their child is finally born their greatest yearning has been satisfied. They may not reach all their career or money goals, become rich and famous, or even "marry well," but those desires all pale before the in-born need to be a mother or father.

Women, especially, long to hold babies in their arms and be mothers. Many will go to almost any lengths to fulfill their need to have a child. If nature doesn't cooperate, they will undergo lengthy and expensive fertility treatments, or pursue other options such as surrogacy or adoption. You might say women have a burning desire to be a parent. But wanting to be a parent isn't exclusive to women. Men, too, feel the need to build a family. They are most fulfilled when wives and children grace their homes. They take pride in their families.

And when we grow as parents, we become better people. In the process of helping our children climb the ladder of childhood and learn attitudes and develop skills to surmount the challenges they find each step of the way, we discover much about ourselves. And we strive to be all we can be.

But to get to that point, we must also overcome the challenges of raising children, of which there are many. We cannot become our best selves without overcoming the obstacles of life. And there is nothing like raising children to put some obstacles in our way! Let's look at the following snapshot of Dana and Patrick to see some of the obstacles in a baby's first year and how becoming a parent will challenge your sense of self from the get-go. After that, we'll examine the ways in which parenthood also helps you to grow up, to mature into a person who feels willing and able, capable and competent, to live life for all it's worth. Through parenting we discover our personal truths, and in so doing become authentic people.

Dana loved being a mother. When her son Samuel was born, it was the happiest day of her life, even better than her wedding day. If she accomplished nothing else, it wouldn't have mattered to her as long as she could have a child, something she'd always wanted to do. She couldn't imagine going through life without becoming a mom. And fortunately, her husband Patrick shared her dream to have a family. Life seemed perfect when Samuel came into the world, a bright-eyed little boy with a full head of dark hair. Dana and Patrick "loved him to pieces."

But then real life hit. Dana realized that life changed after the baby was born. Although Dana loved her young son and gladly accepted the demands of caring for him, she was nonetheless surprised to find that feeling complete didn't mean that her life was perfect. While she was anticipating being a mother and then finally got pregnant, her fantasies were filled with joy and total happiness. And she was sure that her life would remain the same, only enhanced by the birth of a child.

I'm no longer "Karen" or "Mrs. Wilkins." Now they call me "Emma's mom." But you know what? I don't mind a bit! Being Emma's mom is the best and most satisfying part of being me. It's my favorite identity.

—Karen Wilkins, mom of three

"My sunny skies and rainbow dreams of motherhood may have been a little overblown," Dana admits. "Even though I still think Samuel is the best thing that ever happened to me, the day-to-day realities are a little different from what I visualized!" In fact, she hadn't realized how many adjustments she would need to make in the way she lived her life. And she found out that it had been unrealistic to expect that having a child would make life's difficulties less stressful. In fact, becoming a parent can add even more stress to life, as Dana and Patrick discovered. They sometimes felt as if they were losing aspects of what made them who they were; their identities became defined as "Mom" and "Dad." And would there ever be a moment when the baby wouldn't dominate practically all their time? Was the word "carefree" a thing of the past? Would their lives ever return to normal?

Dana and Patrick loved being Mom and Dad. But sometimes they missed those things that made them Dana and Patrick. Could they assume their new roles as parents without losing themselves? Let's take a look at some of the pressures that a baby's first year of life exerts on one's sense of self.

SIX WAYS A BABY WILL CHALLENGE THE WAY YOU SEE YOURSELF

It's a fact: You change when you have a baby. You're no longer the same person you were before becoming a parent. This can certainly be a change for the better, as we all come to realize the truly unconditional love we are capable of when we have a child. But we may mourn the self we were, the things we lose, and the way of life we had. And, of course, we will learn what we cannot do, or do not wish to do, but must! In short, we learn a great deal about ourselves—good and bad!

You Will Feel Incompetent: Every Day Is Like the First Day at a New Job

Your opinion of yourself is based on your estimation of your competence in various aspects of life. If you feel confident that you're a good artist because people buy your artwork, you'll see yourself as talented and capable of using your talent to make a living. If you keep getting promoted at work, you realize that you're good at what you do and that others recognize and reward it. If you consistently win marathons, you know that you're a good athlete and have drive, determination, and a competitive spirit. You'll feel like a winner. It feels great to see yourself as a capable and competent person, and it definitely fuels a positive sense of self. But being a competent artist, manager, or athlete doesn't necessarily translate into being a confident parent. One of the first things you learn about baby's first year is that parenting has a skillset of its own, and that you'll experience a year of feeling like it's your first day on the job!

29

Dana was surprised at how incompetent she felt as a mother. She'd always been a dynamo at the travel agency where she worked and had never doubted her abilities before. Suddenly, with all her worries about Samuel, she no longer felt like an expert. Everything was new to her. She knew which cruise line was the best, which airlines had the most flexible schedules, and how to get the best hotel rates, but standing at his crib at 3 A.M., she had no idea why this little guy was fussy, or what she should or could do about it. She had fed and diapered him, and she'd walked and rocked him for the last hour. But the moment she lay the little thing down, he cried and cried. What should she do?! Feeling so uncertain, even afraid she might not do the right thing for the baby, made her feel very insecure. "Shouldn't I instinctively know these things?" she asked herself.

Coping with a new infant was one thing; coping with her new body was another area in which insecurity ruled the day. In short, nothing fit. It almost killed Dana to shop in the size 10 section when she'd never bought anything beyond a size 8 in her life! It was depressing, and when she didn't feel that she looked her best, it affected her self-confidence. She found herself telling everyone that she'd just had a baby to explain her expanded waistline, as though wearing a size 10 was not acceptable to the rest of the world. "What happened to my self-confidence?" she asked herself time and time again.

Dana's husband Patrick was dealing with his own self-esteem issues. The first time he had to diaper the baby, he put the diaper on backwards! Did the tabs fasten in the front or in the back? Why weren't there any directions? One afternoon, his wife left him with a sleeping baby so she could do some shopping. Dana had told him to warm up a bottle if the baby woke up, but he hadn't thought to ask her how long he was supposed to warm it. What if he burned little Samuel's mouth? Patrick was praying that Dana would get home before Samuel woke from his nap. And what if he started screaming and Patrick didn't know how to calm him down? He'd feel terrible if Dana called to check in and heard the baby crying in the background.

Questions for Discussion

❀ Are you concerned that you won't be a competent parent? Do you lack confidence in your abilities?

_____

_____

❀ How can you feel more confident about your parenting skills?

_____

_____

❀ Do you worry that your appearance will suffer as a result of pregnancy or parenthood?

_____

_____

❀ How can you feel better about your appearance?

_____

_____

Take Action!

Think about those things that you feel skilled at. Then remember the early days when you were just starting out with them. Perhaps you're a good writer, but were you always that way? Probably not. Although you had some natural ability, when you look back at your early writings you may chuckle at seeing how green you were. But with practice and perseverance, you became accomplished in your field. Parenting is the same way. Yes, you're going to make mistakes. But you have the innate ability to learn and grow as a parent. Parenting is a work in progress. As we tackle the challenges that come our way, we develop more confidence in our abilities.

Once Dana's friend picked Samuel up and he started crying, but the tears instantly stopped flowing when he was handed back to Dana. "Wow!" Dana thought, surprised. "I really know how to please my baby after all! He doesn't need anything great from me. He just wants his mommy." It made Dana feel really good about herself. And real-

> *For every woman who lost her baby weight, there are a hundred of us whose bodies will never be the same again. The pregnancy weight never quite goes away, and just when you have the energy to exercise again, your child refuses to sit in the stroller. Combine that with the warm, salty French fries toddlers never seem to finish and the cut-off crust from every PB&J you make, and most of us will never see a size 6 again. So as the woman who considers herself living proof that you can live an absolutely fabulous life and still be twenty pounds overweight, I've decided to give myself a gift . . . This year I'm giving myself the gift of mediocrity, at least when it comes to my body.*
>
> —Lisa Earle McLeod, syndicated newspaper columnist and author of *Forget Perfect*

izing that Samuel wanted her whether she was a size 2 or a 22 gave her a new perspective on her priorities. Dana also tried to praise Patrick for his efforts. When he put mismatched clothes on Samuel, she knew to keep her mouth shut and be grateful that he wanted to share in the parenting duties. She didn't want Patrick to doubt his abilities. She knew that some of her friends' husbands felt that child rearing was "women's work," and she was pleased that Patrick didn't share that attitude. As Samuel thrived, Dana and Patrick felt more confident about their parenting skills. They knew that when a second child arrived, they'd feel like experts!

Neurosis Will Appear, Self-Doubt Will Rule the Day, and You'll Become an Obsessive-Compulsive!

If you never considered yourself a worrywart, you may find yourself undergoing a personality change when you become a parent, in that your heart will be burdened in more ways than you could have known. Suddenly, the littlest concerns are blown up into major what-ifs! If it's snowing outside, you worry that the baby's not dressed warmly enough. If the baby has a cough, you instantly suspect pneumonia. If your child doesn't have a 300-word vocabulary by the time she's two, you're concerned that she might be "slow." Especially with your first child, you don't know what's considered normal, so you wonder if you're doing the right things for her. How can this helpless child possibly fend for herself in this dangerous world? And what if you fail to protect her? It's a time of fears and doubts.

Dana had always prided herself on her even temperament. When things got stressful at the travel agency, she was always the first person to calm everyone down and assure them that "things will get done!" She never would have considered herself a worrier. But now with baby Samuel, things were personal. And Dana found that she had less control over circumstances than she would have liked. If she had a deadline at work, she could work overtime and enlist extra help to get the situation under control. But when Samuel developed a cough, she felt totally helpless to manage things. She worried—a lot! "What if it turns into pneumonia?" "Should I have taken him to the doctor sooner?" "Am I overreacting?" And then there were the bigger concerns: Would she make the right decisions for him? What if Samuel's growing attachment to the sitter meant he wasn't completely bonding to her, his real mom? And what about his crying when she left him with the sitter: How long did he miss her, and was this hurting him in some way? Would she be a good mother? What if she messed up his upbringing? Would he be safe at someone else's house? What if the sitter didn't buckle him tightly? Would she drive more carefully with her young son in the car? The what-ifs mounted in Dana's mind. She never expected to be so consumed with worries after spending her life thus far being "the level-headed one." And she'd never felt such a constant worry—one that felt more like heartache.

> *Now that I'm a dad, every decision is like solving the mystery of the atom.*
>
> —Greg Kinnear

Questions for Discussion

❀ Would you consider yourself a worrier or a "go-with-the-flow" kind of person?

_____

_____

❀ Has being a parent affected how much you worry?

_____

❋ In what ways is worrying productive? In what ways is worrying destructive?

Take Action!

Allow yourself ten minutes a day to worry. Write your worries down in a notebook and put it away in a drawer. Then don't allow yourself to worry the rest of the day! When you start to worry, remind yourself that you can think about it during your designated ten minutes the next day. If you're religious, release your worries to a Higher Power and allow Him to take them off your shoulders. Remind yourself that you'll be a better parent if you're not stressed out with worry.

Don't tell me that worry doesn't do any good. I know better. The things I worry about don't happen.

—Anonymous

Although Dana could never completely erase her worries, she resolved to put them in perspective. She wasn't going to let them rule her life! The next time a worry entered her mind, she replaced it with a positive thought. For example, when she worried that she wasn't giving Samuel enough to eat, she reminded herself that the doctor had been very pleased with his weight at his last visit. When she worried that daycare would have a negative affect on Samuel, she remembered how much the babysitter loved him and had told her how much she missed him on the weekends! By replacing negative thoughts with positive ones, Dana was able to keep her worrying to a minimum.

You'll Wish You Had an M.D. in Pediatric Medicine, a Ph.D. in Child Psychology . . . and a Free Ticket to Maui!

Most people naturally assume that the way they were raised was the "right way," the way that everyone else should be raised! They're usually in for a big shock when they marry someone who had a very different upbringing. Married couples are often surprised to find that they don't always think alike in the parenting department. After all, the way they were raised is what made them who they are, so having to change things with their own child is like denying a part of themselves. Impending and new parents also make the mistake of assuming that responding to their baby's needs will be instinctual—only to discover that instinct is not enough. The real question becomes: What does this child need to best grow into a happy and healthy being? Dana and Patrick frequently had to work through finding the answer to this question together.

> *Before I married, I had six theories about bringing up children. Now I have six children and no theories.*
>
> —John Wilmot, Earl of Rochester

Dana and Patrick had never imagined that parenting wouldn't come naturally. When Samuel cried, Patrick instinctively went to pick him up. But he was shocked when Dana reprimanded him for doing it so quickly. "If you get him that fast," she told him, "he'll never learn to soothe himself. He'll have us constantly running around to meet his every need. Next time, let him cry for a few minutes." Although Patrick could see Dana's point, he couldn't stand to listen to Samuel cry. His own mother had always come running every time he yelled for her. Wasn't it

> *The thing that impresses me most about America is the way parents obey their children.*
>
> —King Edward VIII

his job as a parent to make sure that Samuel was happy? "Yes," agreed Dana, "but our job is also to make sure that Samuel learns the skills he needs to succeed in life. We can't always be there for him when he gets older. It's never too early to start teaching him that lesson." Dana and Patrick were beginning to realize that caring for a child was more complicated than they had thought. They discovered that there are different ways to parent, and that none of them were necessarily "right" or "wrong." But both Dana and Patrick had to look inward to examine

It's important for Tom and me to present a united front for our child. If I think he's too hasty to put our daughter in time-out, I address it with him later instead of undermining him in front of Jenna. Our daughter knows she can't play us against each other. And after Tom and I have discussed it, he usually understands my viewpoint.

—Nancy Franklin, mother of three-year-old Jenna

how they really felt about these kinds of issues. They realized that they came from very different backgrounds and that their parenting philosophies didn't always mesh. But who was right—Dana or Patrick? Both quickly became very interested in knowing what is best. "We must have bought ten baby books that first year!" laughs Dana. The good news is that both of them learned a lot about how to get the best results in caring for their little boy.

Questions for Discussion

● Do you think that being a good parent comes naturally or must be learned?

_____

_____

● Do you believe you have good parenting instincts? Why or why not?

_____

_____

● Have you and your partner discussed your parenting philosophies? Have you clarified them in your own mind?

_____

_____

● How will you and your partner resolve differences in parenting styles?

_____

_____

● Did you find yourself reading more books from the experts than you had anticipated?

_____

_____

> **Take Action!**
>
> Talk to your partner about the way you were raised. Were your parents heavy disciplinarians? Were they strict or permissive? Did you get spankings? Did they expect you to earn your own money? Then talk about whether you want to raise your child in the same way. Perhaps you feel your parents were too tough on you and you want to parent with a lighter hand. Listen to how your partner was raised and how he or she wants to raise your child. Set the ground rules early so that you parent with a united front. It's better to tell your partner now that you don't believe in spanking rather than at the moment your child first gets swatted. Discussing these issues now will avoid conflicts in the future. If your differences are extreme, you may want to consider counseling together.

Dana and Patrick began to read their parenting books and discuss them. They also shared how they had been raised so each would understand the other's point of view. Then they considered which solutions would really be best for Samuel. For example, Patrick understood how important it was to Dana to let Samuel work at self-soothing, so he agreed to react less quickly and busy himself with another task so as not to be tempted to run into the baby's room. The day he found Samuel quietly playing with his "blankie" in his crib after a nap, he realized that Dana had been right to give him some time to himself. The result was a happier baby—and great team parenting!

You'll Miss Your Freedom—"Will There Ever Be Time Just for Me?"

According to *Parenting* magazine (February 2006), "Ninety percent of moms say they don't have enough time for themselves. When they do take some 'me' time, 23 percent feel too guilty to enjoy it.

> *Some people think football is a matter of life and death. I don't like that attitude. I can assure them it is much more serious than that.*
>
> —Bill Shankly

But 19 percent say they 'do it, love it, and deserve it.'" And you should, too! Your interests apart from your child are part of who you are. Therefore, it can feel like a great loss when you no longer have the freedom to pursue them. But with a little creativity and patience, you can do it.

When Patrick's friend Derek called with last-minute tickets to a baseball game, Patrick was ready to go! "Hey, honey, guess what!" he exclaimed to Dana, ready to share his enthusiasm with her. In the past, she would have said, "Great! Have a wonderful time!" But this time, the response was different: "But, Patrick," she reminded him, "I'm supposed to run the charity auction tonight. You promised to stay home with Samuel, remember?" Indeed, Patrick had forgotten. "Couldn't you get someone else to run the auction?" he asked. "Not at the last minute," replied Dana. "Besides, you got to have drinks with your friends last Friday. Don't I deserve a little time to do something I love?" Patrick knew Dana was right. Still, he couldn't help resenting it a little when he had to give up the tickets. In fact, these days it seemed like the only way he got to enjoy the sports he loved was by watching them on TV and trying to catch the commentary over the baby's cries.

Questions for Discussion

✿ Do you think your freedom was curtailed when you become a parent?

_____

_____

✿ How will you handle any resentment at being stuck at home with the baby?

_____

_____

✿ Have you and your partner discussed how you can accommodate each other's need to pursue personal interests?

_____
_____

❀ Why is it important to not totally do away with "me time"?

_____
_____

> **Take Action!**
>
> Make a list of the things you'll lose when you become a parent. Will you be seeing fewer movies? Not spending as much time with your friends? Giving up a favorite hobby? Compare lists with your partner. Cross off the things you'll miss least ("I was getting burned out on playing baseball anyway") and keep the one or two things that really mean the most to you ("Going to my Bible study is important to my spiritual growth"). Then work out ways in which you can continue these activities ("If you watch the baby while I go to church on Thursday evenings, you can still enjoy bowling on Fridays when I'm home"). Coming to agreement about these things will help diminish any guilt you'll feel at leaving your partner to care for the baby. And you'll feel more fulfilled knowing that you don't have to give up all of the activities that you enjoy.

Patrick asked himself this question: Which was ultimately more important to him, his perceived freedom or fatherhood? The answer was easy. Besides, he knew that Samuel's total dependence wouldn't last forever. Sure, he was going to miss a few ball games right now. But there would always be more ball games, and in a few years

> *He who looks outside dreams; he who looks inside wakes.*
>
> —C.G. Jung

he could enjoy them with his son! Although Patrick still regretted not being able to accept his friend's ticket—after all, the seats were "awesome!"—he was proud to tell his friend, "Sorry, my 'daddy duties' call!" Saying that felt good for his sense of self, and whenever he did feel slighted, he quickly recalled the time when he had really wanted to become a father. He still got a thrill every time he said the words "my son." Giving up time with others for time with Samuel was more than a good trade.

You'll Have to Learn How to Cope with Tedious, Mundane, and Boring

When you were planning and dreaming about your life's work, chances are great that it didn't include scrubbing diaper pails and trying to make someone burp! What we do is a big part of who we are. It helps to form our self-concept and our sense of our own importance. But parenting duties aren't prestigious by any means. It's tough to feel self-actualized when you're up to your elbows in "spitty rags" and dirty diapers, as Dana realized.

Dana had always found her work rewarding, and her raises and her clients' praise affirmed her importance to her company. But the work she did at home was another story. She didn't get any money for scrubbing the spit-up stains out of her shirts, and nobody praised her for finally getting rid of Samuel's diaper rash! In fact, sometimes Dana had to admit that she almost dreaded going home to the extra piles of laundry and the dirty baby bottles in the sink. Her job as a mother was definitely lacking in glamour compared to her job as a travel agent. It was a humbling experience for Dana.

Questions for Discussion

❀ Are you the kind of person who needs a lot of "stroking" for your efforts, such as through financial compensation or compliments?

_____

_____

❀ Do you see your duties at home as drudgery, or unfulfilling?

_____

_____

❀ How can you convince yourself that the work you do at home has value?

_____

_____

> ### Take Action!
> You don't need to rely on others to praise you for your accomplishments. Set up a reward system for yourself! The next time you conquer a day's worth of laundry, reward yourself with a cup of your favorite tea and watch the episode of your favorite show that you taped and haven't gotten around to watching. Recognize that your contributions to your home and family are just as valuable as your other accomplishments. Reward yourself for a job well done!

Dana made a list of all the things her mother used to do for her, such as baking homemade cookies, sewing on loose buttons, and throwing fun birthday parties. She realized that this unpaid work had been what she cherished most. It didn't matter that her mother was good at her job or bought her pretty things. It was the way she took care of her that was so priceless. When Dana saw how much worth her job at home really had, she began to see doing these things for her family as a privilege. Doing the laundry and washing dishes were no longer chores she had to do. They were things she wanted to do to take care of her family.

> _Cleaning your house while your kids are still growing is like shoveling the walk before it stops snowing._
>
> —Phyllis Diller
> in Phyllis Diller's
> Housekeeping Hints

You'll Have to Act Like a Grown-Up

If you still feel like a kid at heart, nothing makes you feel more grown-up than becoming a parent. This is especially true for men, who have a particular passion for "toys"! Some parents worry that having to be responsible and mature now will take all the fun out of life. They'll just become "old" in attitude the way their parents seemed to them. But take heart: As much as you'll have to give up many of your childish ways and impractical possessions, you'll soon discover new ways to explore the child within you, which we'll address later in this chapter.

The day that Patrick traded in his Corvette for a minivan was the hardest day of his life—at least, it felt that way to him! When Dana was pregnant with Samuel, she pointed out to Patrick that the whole family wouldn't fit in his car. "So, we'll take your car," he suggested. But that would mean that Dana would always have to take Samuel to the sitter. And what if her car was in the shop? They'd have to spend money on a rental. Besides, Patrick had indulged his passion for a sports car for three years. "Isn't it time to be a little more responsible now?" Dana reminded him. "I also think the motorcycle should go. We won't have as much time to ride it on the weekends, and we can't do it with a baby anyway. Besides, I worry about your safety on that thing—I want you to be Patrick's daddy for a very long time!" It was time to grow up . . . and Patrick wasn't sure he liked it!

> *It goes without saying that you should never have more children than you have car windows.*
>
> —Erma Bombeck

Questions for Discussion

❀ What "toys" will have to go now that you're a parent or parent-to-be?

_____

_____

❀ Do any of your activities seem irresponsible now that you're a parent? Will you be giving them up?

_____

_____

❀ Do you feel a little resentful that you must act more parental and less carefree?

_____

_____

❀ Do you worry that you'll have less fun now that you must adopt a more mature attitude?

_____

_____

> ### Take Action!
> Start hanging out with other new parents and families. You'll soon find that being more responsible doesn't mean having less fun! Being a responsible person doesn't mean that life becomes limited. It just means you find different ways of having a good time! You'll be amazed at the exciting new things you'll find to do!

Once Patrick saw the new crop of SUVs on the market, he realized he didn't have to look like an old fuddy-duddy driving one. He actually found himself getting excited about a new car when he realized he could get a sunroof, a CD player that accommodated eight CDs at a time, and a global positioning system. This could be a fun new toy for Patrick after all! At the same time, its safety features gave him peace of mind. He knew his family would be better protected than in his sports car. Who wouldn't want that for his family? And when the couple down the street invited them (including the baby!) to join them and their three kids for Super Bowl Sunday, Patrick and Dana had a great time! They realized that they could still have fun in spite of their increased responsibilities for Samuel.

Becoming a mother makes you a grown-up. You're all they have. They trust you, they need you. That's all they want. They want to be loved, protected and supported.

—Celine Dion

43

SIX WAYS A BABY WILL CHANGE
YOU FOR THE BETTER

So your freedom will be curtailed, your sense of self gets a thorough review, you'll be saddled with menial jobs 24/7 . . . yes, becoming a parent can be tough on your fragile sense of self. But nurturing children is also an exercise in perfecting our own nature. As we address the many challenges described above, we become a greater version of ourselves, courtesy of being a parent. And what we learn along the way will be equivalent to a PhD—in Life 101.

You'll Feel Complete . . . and Your Heart Will Be Full

Many people find that if they always felt that something was missing from their lives, having a child was it. They feel whole, as if they've completed the rest of the circle that makes up themselves. They no longer quest for the perfect career, the perfect marriage, or the perfect body—they have what they need most to solidify their identity.

> *Motherhood is absolutely necessary. It completes a woman. What is a woman without children?*
>
> —Shaina NC, Indian fashion designer

"The last piece of the puzzle fell into place when I had Samuel," Dana said. "I became a mother. I simply felt complete, as if I'd fulfilled my destiny as a woman. My heart was full." Because Dana had grown up as an only child with a single mother, she often felt her family was incomplete. They'd lived in an apartment, so she hadn't even been able to get a pet! With her marriage and then Samuel's arrival, Dana finally had the family she'd always envisioned. The hole in her heart was gone, replaced by her all-encompassing love for her child. And Dana relished her wonderful new identity as Mom!

Questions for Discussion

❀ Have you ever felt that something was missing from your life?

_____

_____

❀ Do you long to build a family of your own?

_____

_____

❀ Did you dream about one day being called "mother" or "father"?

_____

_____

❀ In what ways does having a child complete you?

_____

_____

Take Action!

Go ahead, buy one of those cheesy necklaces that say "Mom" or a t-shirt that says "World's Best Dad." Wear them proudly! Revel in this new facet of your identity. Let the world know that you're thrilled to be a parent—and you feel important.

You'll Discover the Greatest Love of Your Life

Most people love somebody, whether it's a spouse, parents, or even a pet. But all those loves pale in comparison to the way you feel about your child. You discover that you have the capacity for tremendous love, one that will open up your heart and play havoc with your emotions. Were you amazed to see your spouse cry when your child was born? That's the first sign that you've both just experienced the greatest love of your life.

> _The work of life is to grow closer to who we really are, closer to the image of the person we know ourselves to be deep down. Nothing does that better than raising a child._
>
> —Arlene Burres

Dana was amazed at the depth of love she felt for Samuel. She had never felt such unconditional love. Even when Samuel misbehaved, shunned her affections, or seemed to prefer his dad, Dana was always forgiving. She couldn't even say that about her relationship with Patrick! But with Samuel, she knew that no matter what path he took in life, she would always love him with a full heart. The only love she could compare it to was the love she'd been taught about in Sunday school, the love that God the Father felt for her. She'd never thought that this kind of love could truly be possible; now she was convinced.

Questions for Discussion

❋ Do you believe in unconditional love?

_____

_____

❋ Do you think you will always love your child, no matter what he or she does?

_____

_____

❋ How does your love for your child compare to your love for others? For your partner? For your parents? For God?

_____

_____

Take Action!

Write a "love letter" to your child, expressing your great love for her. Then put it away. One day you'll find the best opportunity to give it to her. It may be a time when she's feeling picked on by others, going through a rough adolescence, or suffering through a break-up with a sweetheart. You'll know when the time is best to share this letter with your child.

Your Life Will Be Filled with Meaning

Raising a child gives your life meaning. If you've often felt like a boat that was sailing aimlessly through life without a real purpose, you'll now feel like you have a rudder. This doesn't mean that you're not meant to fulfill other meaningful objectives as well, but you'll be confident that you've been shown at least one true reason for being. You were meant to be this baby's mother or father, and you're now determined to do the best job of it that you can.

> *The secret of success is constancy of purpose.*
>
> —Benjamin Disraeli

Dana knew that being a great travel agent was a worthy goal. She was proud of her accomplishments and felt that she was doing something worthwhile with her life. Still, she asked herself whether, when she neared the end of her life, it would be enough for her to say, "I was a successful travel agent." There had to be more to life than that. There had to be a better reason for her existence. With Samuel's arrival, Dana realized she had found that purpose: to love and raise Samuel to the best of her abilities. On those days when she got tired of trying to be the best at work, she realized that she never grew tired of fulfilling her mission to be Samuel's mom. This gave her a renewed zest for life, as she knew she was living it with purpose!

> *Every artist dips his brush in his own soul, and paints his own nature into his pictures.*
>
> —Henry Ward Beecher

Questions for Discussion

❀ Have you ever wondered what your purpose is?

_____

_____

❀ Have you felt unfulfilled in your other roles, such as the career you always thought would give your life meaning, but hasn't?

_____

_____

❀ Do you think that being a parent and raising a child is a worthy purpose in life?

_____

_____

47

> ### Take Action!
> Think of someone you know whose parenting style you admire. It might be a friend, a sibling, or even your own parent. Ask them to be your parenting mentor. Seek out their "tricks of the trade" and advice. Talk with them about their disciplinary practices, their decision-making processes, their family traditions. Learn to become the parent you admire in them.

You'll See Life Through the Eyes of a Child Again

When was the last time you were really still, just content to sit in a chair and rock? Chances are, this didn't happen until you held your baby in your arms. And it's easy to forget how beautiful sunsets are or how intricate the wings of a butterfly are until your toddler points to them and exclaims, "Wow!" The things we take for granted are all new experiences to a young child, and it's so much fun to see them with fresh eyes again! Your child won't be small for long. Take this opportunity to slow down and, to use an old cliché, "smell the roses"—and we mean that literally as well as figuratively! This is also a good time to relive the things you loved as a child. If you collected trains or dollhouses—things that are now cluttering the closet or were sold long ago at a garage sale—rediscover your passions by sharing them with your child. You'll be reminded of how much fun it is to have an interest in something special. Dana and Patrick also got in touch with their "inner children" when Samuel was born . . .

Knowing others is intelligence; knowing self is true wisdom.

—Tao Te Ching

Patrick and Dana didn't always agree on what to watch on TV. Dana preferred sitcoms and things that made her laugh. Patrick liked to watch sports and crime shows, which Dana couldn't stand. Then Dana started putting on educational programs when she saw that Samuel was excited about animals. After a while, they were all watching Animal Planet together every night. Soon they were laughing over "Stupid Pet Tricks" and debating which animals would be featured. Patrick and Dana discovered new channels they'd never known existed! They also took Samuel to the zoo, where they hadn't gone since they were children themselves. They were amazed to find how much fun they had! They were experiencing a world full of new adventures—through the eyes of their child.

> *Watching cartoons is the ultimate fantasy escape from reality.*
>
> —Kembrew McLeod, assistant professor of communication studies.

Questions for Discussion

❀ What things did you like to do as a kid that you haven't done in years?

_____

_____

❀ Can you see yourself playing with toys, watching cartoons, and singing songs now that you're a parent?

_____

_____

❀ Do you find that you're having more fun and not taking things so seriously now that you're a parent?

_____

_____

Take Action!

Think about something you loved to do as a kid but haven't done in years. Perhaps it's flying a kite, making a macramé necklace, or playing touch football. So . . . why did you stop? Get out the kite, the jute, or the football and rediscover the joy of having fun! Think about things you can do with your own child that gave you pleasure as a kid. Don't miss out on the opportunity to be a kid again.

You'll Develop a Most Spectacular—and Comprehensive—Skillset

Parenting will both teach and test your skills. If you're preparing for a trip and don't have some diversions planned for your son, you're going to be miserable when he gets bored en route and starts to cry. If you arrive at the sign-up station to enroll your daughter in camp and don't have the appropriate health forms, you'll miss out on one of the coveted spots. If you're running errands and forget to restock the diaper bag, you may find yourself in the middle of Macy's with a messy diaper and no option but to return home. Thinking ahead is key if you want to enjoy life with a child . . .

Patrick and Dana had always lived life by the seat of their pants. "When we bought our house," Dana related, "we didn't really research the prices in the area. We knew we wanted that house, so we just paid what they asked. Now, because money is tighter with Samuel in daycare, I wish we had done our homework. I found out the people across the street paid fifteen thousand dollars less for their house, and it's the same model that we have. Can you imagine how many diapers and boxes of formula that would have bought us? It makes me sick now to think how much we overpaid." With Samuel's birth, Dana and Patrick resolved to be more organized. Instead of waiting until her maternity leave ended to look for daycare, Dana started calling places when she was still pregnant to find out what the going rates were. Then she and Patrick visited several places to help them decide what kind of environment they wanted Samuel in. When they found a place they loved, they found out there was a waiting list.

> *Now that I have kids, I live by the calendar. Sarah's activities go on the calendar in red. Jeremy's events are written in blue, and Libby's are in orange. John and I have our own colors, too. Nobody is allowed to write anything on the calendar without consulting me first. And if it isn't on the calendar, it's not going to happen! This system has really helped our family stay sane!*
>
> —Megan Goodall, a busy mother of three

They put their name on the list even before Samuel was born. Fortunately, an opening came up when Dana's maternity leave ended. "You're lucky you got on the list early," they were told. "We had ten more people put their names on the list after you did. You wouldn't have gotten in for at least another year."

Questions for Discussion

❀ Would you consider yourself to be an organized or disorganized person?

_____

_____

❀ Have you ever missed out on an opportunity because you procrastinated or didn't "have it together"? Give an example.

_____

_____

❀ Why is it important to learn better organizational skills when you're a parent?

_____

_____

Take Action!

Buy a small file cabinet and some file folders. Call it your family file. The next time you get information from your daughter's daycare center or cut out some coupons, create a file for each and place them inside. Take the stacks of paper you have around your house and sort them, then put them in labeled files. Designate a place in the house for you and your spouse to place your keys and money every night. This will save you from being late because you're chasing things down. You'll find that with small improvements in organization, there will be less stress in your life—and more time to spend with your family!

You'll Never Feel Alone—or Lonely

Being a parent means you'll always have family in your life. Certainly the memories alone carry you through many tough times. Your own parents may pass away, siblings might move across the country, marriages can end, but you'll always be a mother or father. The world will feel like a less lonely place when you have someone to share it with. Having this link to another human being is much healthier for your sense of self and your emotional well-being. And there is nothing better than a baby's first year to fill your own life. Even her dependence is welcomed. A baby needs you. To be needed is an important contribution to your mental health. Not to mention a good feeling in your heart.

> *An entire life of solitude contradicts the purpose of our being.*
>
> —Edmund Burke

When Dana's mother passed away from cancer, Dana was devastated. Because she was an only child, her mother had been the last of her family. Her father had left and moved overseas when she was young, and was rarely in contact. It was a very lonely time for Dana. But after Samuel was born, Dana realized she had a family again. Even if, heaven forbid, Patrick left her, like her own dad had left her mom, she would always have her child. She'd never be completely alone. It was a comforting feeling for Dana.

Questions for Discussion

❀ Have you ever considered the permanence of having a child? Is it a reassuring feeling or a scary one?

_____

_____

❀ Have there been times in your life when you've felt alone? How will this change when you become a parent?

_____

_____

❀ Does it comfort you to know that you'll have a child to take care of you in your old age?

_____

_____

> ### Take Action!
> Although it's a wonderful feeling to know that having a child will help you feel less alone, it's also important to learn to savor solitude and not rely on others' company for your happiness. After all, your child will grow up . . . and may even move many miles away! Dare yourself to eat at a restaurant alone or attend a movie. If you have a day to yourself, resist the temptation to pick up the phone. Spend a quiet day reading or gardening by yourself. Learn to love your own company as much as you love that of your husband or child.

CONCLUSION

Although we seem to be always doing things for our children and giving to them—and this is especially true in that first year of baby's life—we get much in return. Parenthood can be a major paradigm shift, motivating us to move beyond our own self-centered concerns and to care deeply about the needs of another. It can help us focus more clearly on the meaning of our own personal journey through time and keep us from sleepwalking through life. In the process of helping our children climb the ladder of childhood, and learn attitudes and develop skills to surmount the challenges found on each step, we discover much about ourselves.

Three

Love, Marriage—and a Baby Carriage: Surviving and Thriving as a Couple

> Having children will test your marriage in numerous ways . . . but as you overcome the challenges and embark on the joys together, you'll find that becoming parents is also the best thing that ever happened to your marriage!

The first year of parenthood presents tremendous changes and challenges for a couple, even if they have been together for some time and feel ready for a child. For sure, your marriage will change after you have children. It will never be the same again! We guarantee it. Some things are so much more wonderful: the new depth of love you'll feel for your children, the bond between you that strengthens as you commit to raising them together, and the pleasure taken in the fulfillment of a lifelong dream to become a parent. But stressors will test your relationship: sleep deprivation and increased demands on your time; fewer shared activities and goals fulfilled; and a diminished sex life. One or both of you may even feel relegated to second place as the little ones consume all your time and attention. It will take extra effort to preserve the couple you were before the baby arrived, and at the same time forge a new relationship as a family. From constantly fulfilling the time-consuming caretaking needs of an infant to losing the in-dependence and time alone that you once shared as a couple, all can take their toll on a relationship. Unless communication and patience are practiced regularly, even the best of relationships will feel the strain, as Steve and Anna learned upon the arrival of Madeleine Rose and Tristan to the family.

> *Having a first child is like throwing a hand grenade into a marriage.*
>
> —Nora Ephron

Steve and Anna considered themselves soul mates. They met in college, married shortly after graduation, and spent the next eight years building their careers—Steve as an accountant for a corporate accounting firm and Anna as a reporter and on-air personality for a local TV station. After four years of renting a loft in the bustling downtown section of town, a lifestyle they described as "the only way to live," they began to think of having a family. They looked at homes and made the decision to buy a large old Victorian house and renovate it from the ground up. While the work on their home took more time and money than they'd bargained for, both Steve and Anna discovered they enjoyed this project, and found it a wonderful way to spend quality time together. Room by room, they planned, worked, and created. Nearly a year and a half into the remodeling, when they agreed that "this room would be great for a nursery," they began to talk more seriously about having a family. A year later, their baby daughter was born.

"Pregnancy was such an awesome experience," Anna confided. "From the moment we confirmed we were expecting, our lives took on a sudden new joy that we couldn't have known. And it united us like nothing we'd ever experienced. Steve was with me at every doc-tor's appointment. We decorated the nursery together, attended pre-natal classes, and shopped together for things the baby would need. It was so amusing to watch my husband look over car seats with the intensity of buying health insurance! We made list after list after list of baby names, and then agreed to name our daughter Madeleine Rose, after our grandmothers. The birth of our baby was such a great time in my life, and his. Our baby was a dream come true for both of us."

Although both Anna and Steve admit that the first year with Madeleine Rose was tougher than they had expected, they were eager to have a second child to complete their family. Baby Tristan was the little boy they had always wanted, but they were surprised to find that things got a lot more complicated with a second child in the house! Says Anna, "While there were huge changes in our lives during Madeleine Rose's first year, nothing could have prepared us for the second baby's first year. With the first baby, I took off three months and then returned to work. My bosses at the TV station were really happy for me, and even allowed me to develop a continuing segment of 'parenting tips for new mom and dads.' I was able to bring Madeleine Rose to work and set up a little crib in my office. But with Tristan's arrival, that just wasn't an option. It's a whole different ballgame trying to bring two kids to work! For one thing, juggling a baby and a toddler is nothing like I'd imagined. You have no idea what it is like with two kids in the car, both under the age of five! The toys you need, the supplies you need, the ability to both attend to the road and the safety measures within the car . . . these are more than a challenge. And with two children, there's just no downtime. When one's asleep, the other's awake. If I thought my free time was limited with just one child, those days seem like a walk in the park now that I have two. Steve and I had a lot of adjustments to make after we had Tristan."

This time around, Anna reluctantly decided to take a one-year unpaid leave of absence from her job. Unfortunately, it came at a time when Anna's career was on an upswing, with a recent promotion and rumors of the lead anchor job, but she just couldn't swing the added demands of her new job and the demands of her family at home. So she put her career dreams on hold. But it wasn't long before the loss of income was sorely missed, especially since they had traded in a paid-off car for a new minivan and the old house still needed some things that couldn't be put on hold—like extra space heaters in the baby's room. "Does life exist after a baby?" Anna quipped, and then answered her own question, "No!" Of course, it's not that life doesn't exist, but it's dramatically changed, especially when a second child comes along. And these changes—and our response to them—often catch us off guard. Even Steve was surprised by his adjustment issues. Because he was now the only one earning the money, he began to question Anna about expenditures and reminding her of the importance of not spending frivolously. Anna, of course, resented him second-guessing her judgment, and was surprised when, after all, the money she did spend was primarily centered on the needs of the children.

"I've done a perfectly fine job managing our finances until now," she said. "Suddenly, my husband's telling me that Tristan doesn't need another sleeper—how can he not notice that three- to six-month clothes don't fit an eight-month-old?—and he's questioning whether our son really needed to go to the doctor when he developed that cough—after telling me just the other day that someone at work had come down with walking pneumonia! And we really need to start looking for preschools for Madeleine Rose now that she's three. Money, money, money . . . it seems like it's the center of all of our issues now."

> *Nothing can prepare you for motherhood. You can feel 120 percent ready but until that baby's in your arms, you have no clue.*
>
> —Gretchen Carlson, FOX News Anchor

Other bones of contention also came between the easy sweetness that Steve and Anna once took for granted—a couple who once described themselves as wanting a house full of kids. "Anna used to be meticulous," said Steve. "Now I come home from work and there are two days' worth of baby bottles stacked in the sink, our three-year-old's toys are strewn everywhere, and sometimes Anna's still in her pajamas! What happened to the woman who took pride in her house and her appearance? Worst of all, she talks constantly about whether formula X works better than formula Z. If the baby is happy and eating, what's the big deal? It seems like her entire existence revolves around the kids. I can't remember the last time she handed off the kids to her mom, cooked me a favorite meal, put on perfume, and lit the candles. I love our kids as much as she does, but we need some time without them, too."

"How insensitive can he be?" Anna retorted. "You don't just 'get rid of the kids,' even for an evening! Of course, I care about our relationship, but frankly, I'm exhausted after caring for a baby and a three-year-old all day. And I'm the one who's been getting up at night with the baby, and going to Madeleine Rose when she's having a bad dream, needs a glass of water, or is ill. I feel like Steve is jealous of the attention that the children need from me. Who's the baby now?"

Clearly, even after having gone through the adjustments of a baby's first year with the birth of Madeleine Rose, Steve and Anna were experiencing even more strain with the arrival of a second child.

Steve and Anna's predicament is not uncommon. Although they both shared a deep and abiding love for their children, they found that the needs of a new baby once again added stress and strain to their relationship. After many years of marriage, the couple had established a life that worked for the two of them—and then the three of them after their daughter's arrival—but now the relationship needed to work for all four of them—a greater challenge, indeed.

> _If you are too tired to do anything together, you have no advantage over couples who don't want to do anything together._
>
> —Bryce Winke

Let's take a look at some of the pressures that a baby's first year of life exerts on a marriage, and ways you can work toward moving the pendulum from confinement, confusion, and chaos back to fun, reward, and growth.

FIVE WAYS A BABY WILL ADD CHALLENGE, CHANGE, AND CHAOS TO YOUR MARRIAGE

It's not uncommon for couples to go through a "mourning period" after a baby arrives, even if they're totally thrilled that they've become parents. They may not even realize that they are in mourning, but the fact remains: They no longer enjoy a sense of independence and "just the two of us." When the second child arrives, many couples mistakenly believe it's "been there, done that," and the pressures will be fewer. They are often surprised to find that "baby makes four" can be even more complicated! Of course, there are great joys in having a second child—your family often feels complete now that there are two children—but with greater parental responsibilities come more concessions and challenges for parents. It is another time of growth and challenge for a marriage.

Sleep Deprivation Will Take a Toll on Your Patience

Does it seem as if you and your spouse are always snapping at each other lately? Sleep deprivation will do that to you! It's easy to blow small things out of proportion when you can barely deal with the situation in front of you. When nearly every waking hour is spent being on call for meeting the demands of a small child—or two—it's no wonder we get cranky. And parents frequently find more to argue about when it comes down to issues of raising children. For instance, you may not agree with your partner's decision to let the baby "cry it out," or he may not honor the routine you've worked so hard to put in place, and wakes the baby after you've spent an hour feeding, bathing, and rocking her to sleep. Sleep deprivation is sure to take a toll on your ability to cope, so it's not surprising that arguments arise, as Anna and Steve found out.

> *For two people in a marriage to live together day after day is unquestionably the one miracle the Vatican has overlooked.*
>
> —Bill Cosby

Anna really needed eight hours of sleep, but now that she was up every few hours with the baby, she found herself, in her words, "so emotional" and "short-tempered." Not to mention, in Steve's words, "crabbier and crabbier." One afternoon, while preparing a bottle for the baby, who was screaming at the top of his lungs while the phone was ringing and Madeleine Rose was demanding a cookie, Anna noticed the towels Steve had attempted to toss in the laundry room—missing it by several feet! Seething, Anna vowed to nail Steve on it the second he walked through the door after work. Luckily, she caught herself: "Where has the girl gone who once laughed at Steve's chronic untidiness?" she wondered. Now she resented the fact that he was just adding one more thing to her to-do list—and she couldn't get things done as it was! Anna knew she was overreacting because she hadn't had enough sleep, but she frankly resented having to allow Steve a good night's sleep so he could be fresh for work and yet he wasn't grateful enough to pick up his clothes! Anna's growing impatience with the "little things" was taking a toll on their marriage.

But Steve, too, had his own list of irritations. Why did Anna always switch the caps on the bottles after Steve had put them together just because they weren't color coordinated? Was it really that important that the yellow bottle have a yellow cap, and the blue bottle have a blue cap? It seemed so petty to Steve. And why did she have to keep the baby monitor on so loud? Frankly, it was keeping Steve up even when the baby was sleeping. Surely they'd hear the baby's cries if the monitor were turned down a bit. Steve was tired of battling it out with Anna as they each turned the volume up and down, up and down all night.

> *Marriage—as its veterans know well— is the continuous process of getting used to things you hadn't expected.*
>
> —Tom Mullen

Questions for Discussion

❀ Are you feeling overtired because the baby is cutting into your sleep time, your reading time and, well, every waking moment? Are you in need of some time to yourself?

_____

_____

❀ Do you or your partner resent the other getting more sleep? How can you make this more equitable?

_____

_____

❀ Do you find yourself being crankier because you're exhausted and have lost control of your once-prized independence? How do you take it out on your partner?

_____

_____

❀ Have you shared your feelings with your partner? What is your plan for resolving these issues?

_____

_____

❀ What are two ways you each can have a reprieve from the demands of parenting?

_____

_____

> **Take Action!**
>
> Talk to each other about ways you can get more sleep. If one of you is getting enough sleep during the week in order to be well rested for a job, then allow the other partner to have a good night's sleep on the weekends. Or agree that certain things on the to-do list will get put on hold to enable the primary caregiver to rest while the children nap. Most of all, recognize that your grouchiness is due to lack of sleep and increased demands on your time: Be more tolerant of each other and remind yourself that this stage won't last forever. (It only seems like it!)

I went looking for my husband to tell him how annoyed I was that he left his dirty dishes in the sink once again for me to put in the dishwasher. I found him in our daughter's room. He was lightly stroking her arm with his fingertip as she slept and humming a little lullaby. He had such a look of pure love and pride in his eyes. The dirty dishes were quickly forgotten.

—Karen Kay, new mother

It's a mistake to think that your partner will see things the same way you do. Rarely do couples see eye to eye on every issue. The ways we respond to things do not require total compatibility, but rather the loyalty and commitment necessary to deal constructively with differences, whether it's handling finances or taking care of towels-on-the-floor sorts of issues.

Although Steve will probably have a hard time breaking his habit of throwing his laundry on the floor, the bigger issue here is consideration for Anna's feelings. Steve and Anna drew up a list of their household chores and prioritized those things that they felt must get done and those that could slide for now. Then each took on the responsibility for a fair share of the list. To Anna's delight, Steve agreed to take full charge of Madeleine Rose and Tristan for two straight hours on Sunday afternoons so that she could get a relaxing bath and a nap to be refreshed for the coming week. It improved Anna's mood tremendously! And made her feel that Steve genuinely cared about how she was faring, and that he understood her need for time away from the continual dependency needs of the new baby.

Intimacy Will Suffer (It's Mostly "Quickies" from Here On Out!)

If the sexual excitement of your pre-baby days seems like a distant dream, you've entered the realm of parenthood. Experts say there are only two things you should be doing in your bed: having sex and sleeping. After having a baby, the percentage of time spent on each activity dips heavily to the side of sleeping—or, at least, attempting to get some rest! And even when you decide to give sex a go, your mind is focused on every noise coming from the baby monitor, or you're worried that the three-year-old will come barging into your bedroom because she's too scared to sleep in her own. You're hoping you can just get away with a quickie, or maybe even use the kids as an excuse to put things off for another night.

Steve and Anna had enjoyed a good sex life before having children, but for the first time in their marriage Anna was no longer interested. Once her weary body hit the mattress, the last thing she could think about was summoning the energy for sex! Anna also felt self-conscious about her post-baby body. She'd bounced back fairly quickly after having Madeleine Rose, but the second time around her body wasn't rebounding as quickly. Carrying some twenty pounds of post-baby weight, and "leaking" milk whenever her breasts were touched, Anna no longer felt sexy, only "fat and matronly." Where once she used to initiate sex as much as her husband, now she hoped he'd fall asleep before she got into bed. Naturally, Steve noticed, and saw her lack of enthusiasm as a rejection.

> *Happy marriages begin when we marry the ones we love, and they blossom when we love the ones we marry.*
>
> —Tom Mullen

"It's not that I no longer like sex or don't desire my husband," said

Anna. "Every day my intention is to give my husband the green light when we hit the sheets but then, at the end of a very long day, when my head finally hits the pillow, it seems that my body just doesn't want to cooperate and all I want to do is slip into dreamland! The 'right night' just never seems to arrive." And Anna couldn't forget the night when they were just getting intimate and Madeleine Rose suddenly started screaming at the top of her lungs! It turned out that she was only having a nightmare, but still the mood was broken, and Anna worried that this would happen the next time they had sex. She wanted to be there for her children, but she didn't want to let her husband down either.

Questions for Discussion

❀ Are you having less sex now that the baby has arrived? How often did you have it before the baby? And now?

_____

_____

❀ Does one of you resent the other for not being as interested in sex?

_____

_____

❀ How do you and your partner show love and affection without having sex?

_____

_____

❀ Do you feel your relationship has suffered due to your diminishing intimacy? How can you discuss it with each other without pointing fingers?

_____

_____

> **Take Action!**
>
> Be mindful of the important role of intimacy in building togetherness. A couple that strives to serve one another has a greater acceptance level for a nourishing sex life.

A talk was definitely in order for Anna and Steve. Although Anna reassured Steve that she didn't intend to put sex on the back burner for the rest of their lives, she wanted him to understand the very real issues that were going on in her head. The fatigue, her body issues, needing to be on call for the kids— all these things were making it difficult for her to resume an active sex life, at least for now.

According to a poll by Parenting _magazine (February 2006), what parents miss most about married life before kids is . . ._
Time to sleep (late) together: 63 percent
Time for sex: 22 percent
Time for conversation: 15 percent

Although Steve didn't see these issues being as important as Anna did, he was eager to do what he could to get Anna back to feeling more romantic. They agreed on working toward times, especially on the weekends, when Steve could take the kids so that Anna had some time for herself to get in touch with her feminine side, and not just the "mom" side. Steve also agreed that he would take a bigger role in preparing meals for them, and that he'd go the extra mile to do all he could around the house, especially since Anna's time was carefully measured. The demands of breastfeeding and tending to an infant who still didn't sleep through the night taxed Anna's ability to cope. Both Steve and Anna agreed that the state of their marriage was logical and to be expected with the addition of a second child into the mix. Choosing to see the problem as sleep-related helped them realize it was short-term and therefore tolerable. In the meantime, even cuddling together became more important. The goal was to feel united and close, and not to create pressure to have sex. As they made the effort to touch each other more, both found themselves slowly getting back to a more frequent sex life.

Independence Will Be Curtailed—in Other Words, You'll Be Grounded

Long gone are the days when you can throw some clothes in a bag and take off at a moment's notice. Anyplace that you want to go, you need to consider: Is it kid-friendly? How much will it cost for all of us? What kind of supplies do we need? The planning involved is monumental. Some activities will just have to be put on hold until the kids are older, although if your eldest child is of school age, he or she can often lighten the load by playing with a cranky baby or helping with simple chores. Regardless of the children's ages and independence, however, any outings now require much more preparation, as Steve and Anna found.

> _Sometimes I come to bed only to find that my wife has fallen asleep while nursing the baby. I do think that seeing her lie there with our baby in her arms is probably the most beautiful and sexual image I've ever seen._
>
> —Robert Redman, new dad

When Steve's company sent him on a business trip to Las Vegas, the couple decided it was a good opportunity to take a mini-vacation for the whole family. After three hours of packing and nitpicking over what to take, they finally threw the car seat, stroller, Madeleine's toys and books, several suitcases, and a "just-in-case" backpack filled with emergency supplies into the trunk. (On the bright side, when they got to the airport, they were allowed to board first because of the baby!) In the plane, they endured dirty looks all the way to Vegas when the baby cried because his little ears "popped." And Madeleine Rose kept kicking the seat of the passenger in front of her.

When they arrived that evening at the show they had purchased tickets for, they were told in no uncertain terms, "No children allowed!" So they went to dinner instead, where they were seated in the family section. This part of the restaurant was filled mostly with mothers accompanied by two or more small children who hadn't quite mastered the skills of eating or sitting still. This got their own children excited, and soon Madeleine Rose was running all around the restaurant, joyfully exclaiming how much she loved her new doll! And while Madeleine Rose was cute practicing her new "shrill" sound non-stop, Anna was mortified when Tristan threw a fork across the room, barely missing another diner. Needless to say, this dinner out was far from intimate, as Steve and Anna could barely hear each other talk.

> *The greatest tragedy of the family is the unlived lives of the parents.*
>
> —C.G. Jung

On the way back to their room, they passed a casino and spontaneously decided to each put a twenty-dol-lar bill in a machine to see who fared the best. Well, the machine had no more than gobbled up their money—and had yet to spit out their change—before a uniformed policeman escorted them out. (No one under eighteen allowed.) Back in the room, after ordering a crib for the baby, they went to bed. Their sleep was interrupted three times that night because Tristan was fussy from teething. Steve felt like a zombie the next day as he tried to concentrate on his business meet-ings. Anna, in the meantime, tried to take both children to the hotel pool, but after spending an hour dressing them, slathering on sun-screen, and trying to chase down their sunhats, water wings, and pool toys, she was exhausted. So much for a relaxing vacation! The whole trip, in fact, was far from the "fun family experience" that Steve and Anna had hoped for.

Questions for Discussion

❀ What trips and recreational activities do you miss that you used to enjoy?

_____

_____

❀ Are you nervous about leaving the baby with a caretaker? Why?

_____

_____

❀ Do you feel guilty if you schedule something that doesn't include your children? How can you overcome these feelings of guilt?

_____

_____

❀ Are trips more stressful now when there are kids involved? In what ways can you minimize the stress?

_____

_____

> ### Take Action!
> After Anna and Steve's experience in Las Vegas, they learned a few lessons for the future that you can keep in mind: First, trust that your children will be okay with a trusted relative or friend while you and your partner take a trip. They will care for them just as well as you. (If you're breastfeeding, pump bottles ahead of time and have the sitter supplement with formula if your baby tolerates it.) Second, schedule a little vacation for just the two of you several months down the road. Make the tickets nonrefundable—then you'll have to follow through on your plans! (Make sure you have a trusted sitter lined up first.) Start small: Book a room in a nice hotel for one evening, so that you're only away for one night. Once you all survive this first experience, you'll find it easier to schedule longer getaways. And if you must forgo travel for now, don't feel neglected. There really will be time for travel . . . childhood doesn't last forever, and your children won't always want to travel with you!

Anna arranged for her parents to come stay with the children for their wedding anniversary, which was four months away. Then she booked two nights at the bed-and-breakfast where she and Steve stayed on their first vacation together. Although they were nervous at first about leaving Madeleine Rose and Tristan, they relaxed and enjoyed themselves after several calls home reassured them that the kids were doing just fine. In fact, Anna's mother had finally gotten the baby to eat strained peas, and Madeleine Rose was helping Grandpa plant flowers in the garden. Steve and Anna returned home well-rested and holding hands after spending a wonderful weekend together—a trip that went a long way over the next several trying months.

"Just the Two of Us" Will Be History

Most childless couples have little rituals they develop over time. They may take a walk every day after work, cook breakfast together on Saturday mornings, head to the movies every Friday night, or even fold the laundry together! These activities can be a real bonding experience for a couple, something

> _There is so little difference between husbands, you might as well keep the first one._
>
> —Adela Rogers St. John

they look forward to sharing with each other. But these things are often the first to go when children alter the schedule. Either you're too busy now to engage in these activities, or they're not kid-friendly, or one of you has to tend to the children while the other gets things done alone. Interestingly, many men have told us that when their wives became mothers, they often voluntarily took on more traditional roles in the household that were formerly done equally between husband and wife. Perhaps it's the maternal instinct emerging, but some women were suddenly choosier about how things were done around the house, and fathers fell into letting their wives manage the house and kids in order to maintain peace between them. As couples pursue more and more separate activities, they are frequently surprised at how much they miss doing things as a team. But with a little brainstorming they may also find that new rituals can be incorporated that involve the whole family.

Anna and Steve were surprised to find that folding the baby's clothes together was a loving experience and that doing this allowed them to reminisce about special times and plan for times ahead. This time became so valuable that they actually set aside time each week for it.

Before having the children, Steve and Anna loved to get up early on Saturday mornings, drive ten miles out to the country, and mountain bike. This ritual was followed by an outdoor lunch, grocery shopping together, and then stopping to pick out a movie they'd watch later that evening after finishing up their errands and working on the house. They each loved this day together, and they often said in the middle of their hectic weeks, "Only X days until Saturday!" Once Madeleine Rose arrived, the once-cherished Saturday plan simply stopped. Anna told Steve to take a friend and go for a ride, which he did—once. But he could see the resentment in Anna's eyes and felt it was too big a price to pay. And just when Madeleine Rose was getting big enough to ride in a seat on the back of one of their bikes, little Tristan arrived to put these plans on hold once again. In fact, Steve and Anna found that many activities shut down. Soon, they did less and less together. But the resentment remained.

Questions for Discussion

❁ What things do you miss most that you used to do together?

_____

_____

❁ Have you shared with each other how you feel about this?

_____

_____

❁ What are your plans for modifying your activities now that you have a baby so that you can still share time together?

_____

_____

❁ Do you have a timeline for adding your children to the activities you're no longer doing (or is that not possible)?

_____

_____

> **Take Action!**
>
> What is your plan for resuming the activities you once shared as a couple? Make it a priority to spend at least one hour together after the children go to bed. Don't wander off to do separate activities. Share a cup of tea, watch a movie together, or work on a puzzle. Make this time together a necessary part of your schedule each day. You'll soon be looking forward to this special time!

Although Steve and Anna realized that their bikes would have to stay in the garage for now, they bought a tandem jogging stroller and found a park with some great walking trails. Soon they were spending their Saturdays speed-walking at the park with Madeleine Rose and Tristan comfortably ensconced in their new stroller. But the part they liked best was feeding the ducks that congregated in the river that ran through the park. They always took some food with them, and when their exercising was done, the children looked forward to tossing crackers to the ducks. In fact, one of Tristan's first words was "duck"! Although they rued the dust that was gathering on their bikes, the whole family loved the new tradition of the Saturday morning run.

You've got to talk about your resentments before they grow . . . Agree that it's okay to complain. It's natural to miss and mourn life as it once was. Decide that the "grumbling stage" is a good sign: It's time for a babysitter and a good bottle of wine in your favorite little restaurant where you can work toward finding a "replacement" for what was but will be no longer—such as freedom and independence. Get real about the loss, and replace it in ways that incorporate the miracle of the baby who is now part of a bigger and richer life.

—Robin Hightower, new mom

Everything Will Be About the Baby!

So, is there life after kids? Well, yes and no. If you were once Number One in your partner's life, you're probably feeling these days like you've been bumped to the Number Two spot with the arrival of a baby. Just as your wife is poised to give you a loving back massage, the wails from the bedroom take her hands away from you and toward your child. And just as your husband gets ready to fix that leaky faucet you've been asking him to look at for weeks, the baby decides to throw up all over her crib, and you're both scrambling to clean it up and console her. What is that old saying about the best-laid plans? But even though you both understand the necessity of putting the children's needs first, sometimes you still can't help resenting that your own needs aren't getting met.

Steve felt that he had been replaced by his wife's new love—their children. Anna used to make special desserts for him, pick up his suits at the dry cleaners, and look for new additions to his model plane collection. Post-baby, Steve couldn't remember the last time she'd done these things for him. Anna was solely focused on meeting Madeleine Rose and Tristan's many needs, never his. Anna reasoned that she only had so many hands—Steve was an adult and perfectly capable of taking care of himself. Was he asking her to neglect their children just so he could enjoy a little luxurious treatment from her? When it was put like that, Steve knew it sounded childish, but he still couldn't help feeling displaced from his wife's attentions.

Questions for Discussion

❀ Do you feel as if you're getting less attention from your partner now that the baby has arrived?

_____

_____

❀ Do you feel displaced in your partner's affections? Give examples to show why you feel this way.

_____

_____

❀ What things did you used to do for each other that you don't do anymore? How can you make an effort to resume these activities?

_____

_____

> ### Take Action!
>
> Pay attention to the little things. They really do mean a lot! It doesn't take a lot of effort to offer to get your partner a drink if you're going to the kitchen to fix a bottle anyway. Encourage your partner to take a relaxing bath while you watch the children. Let your partner know in little ways how much you still think of him or her. Little efforts can pay off with big results!

Anna never realized that Steve really noticed the little things she had always done for him. After Steve expressed his hurt feelings, Anna vowed to show her husband a little extra attention by leaving notes in his lunch bag and having a glass of wine for the two of them waiting when he got home. These things didn't take her away from the children, but showed Steve that she was thinking of him, too.

I once held a position in my company where I was traveling constantly. I knew that once the baby came, I'd simply need to earn more so my wife could be at home with our son. But with his birth, I don't want to be away from him that much. And I remind myself that in only eighteen years he will be out of the house . . . I don't want to miss out on the joy of being his father.

—Brad Eckmann, new father

FOUR WAYS A BABY WILL CHANGE YOUR MARRIAGE FOR THE BETTER

So Steve and Anna were having huge adjustment problems, especially when a second child was added to the family. Suddenly, they had to find new ways of relating and accommodating their changing needs. And they learned to follow this advice: Give it time. Couples like Steve and Anna find that the first year of parenthood is always the hardest, whether dealing with a first baby, a second, or a third. Accept that your together time will be diminished, your sex life will be put on the back burner, and your own needs may go unmet for a while. And then make new goals for the future: Develop new traditions that include the children, the way Anna and Steve did by going to the park together every Saturday. Make appointments for sex—and stick to them, no matter how tired you feel! Resist the urge to snap at each other, and remember the reasons you got married in the first place. Know that things will get better—and they will. Most of all, focus on the positives of having children—those things that make a marriage better than ever!

> *I look at my child and I realize that nothing in this entire world matters to me more than she does. Nothing.*
>
> —Marty Newman, new father

You'll Realize the Fulfillment of a Dream

Nothing is more bonding than sharing a dream. When athletic teams share the dream of going to the playoffs, they bond together as never before to pursue that dream. The same holds true for married couples. When you mutually choose each other to become the other parent to your children; when you save money, buy a house, and make plans so you can have a family; when you talk about what to name your children and the family traditions you hope to share with them—these are incredible togetherness experiences. A common goal gives a marriage purpose and meaning. It unites the two of you in a powerful way.

Although Steve and Anna shared many dreams together—especially their dream to renovate their home—having Madeleine and Tristan was their biggest dream come true. When they were dating, they used to fantasize about the family they would have—the typical 2.5 kids, the cocker spaniel and the house in the country—and now their dreams were bearing fruit with the births of their daughter and son. Together, they had made it happen, and their children were truly a blessing in their lives. Other dreams would be fulfilled in time, but for the moment they cherished the thought that this particular dream had come true.

> **Take Action!**
>
> Make a list of the dreams you have yet to fulfill. Set goals and timelines for fulfilling them. Recognize that dreams may be put on hold as children arrive, but that doesn't mean they need to be swept aside. Know that having a child is already a dream come true worth celebrating. Trust that your other dreams will come true when the time is right.

Questions for Discussion

❀ What dreams do you and your partner share?

_____

_____

_____

❀ Was having a child a shared dream for the two of you? How do both of you feel now that this particular dream has come true?

_____

_____

_____

___

Everyone wants their marriage to be "romantic." And I'm all for that! But becoming a parent gives greater purpose to marriage than simply as an avenue to happiness and romance. Becoming a parent lends pleasure to marriage and gives me a reason to put the health of my marriage as one of the most important things I will ever do.

—Deborah Ryan, new mother

❀ How can you continue to work on your dreams in the future? Do you believe that they're still possible?

_____

You'll Establish a Bond That Will
Forever Link You Together

But the dream doesn't stop with the goal just to have children. Married couples continue to bond through the goal of continuing to give their children the best life possible. They work together as a couple to ensure that the family they've created thrives and prospers. Having children—and wanting them to grow up healthy and happy—is a goal that will unite you for the rest of your lives.

Steve and Anna now had a common mission: to raise and love their children to the best of their abilities. They both wanted to give Madeleine and Tristan a happy childhood, to raise them with values, morals, and self-confidence, to grow them into adults who would make valuable contributions to society. Their children were their new project, one that would take precedence over any goals they had established in the past. Although they had once aimed to buy a summer home by the lake some day, that goal would be put on hold a little longer while the realities of raising their children dealt with. But Anna and Steve were okay with this sacrifice because they knew that the goal to raise their children to the best of their abilities was now their highest priority.

Questions for Discussion

● What dreams and goals do you have for your children?

_____

_____

● Have you and your partner discussed your parenting philosophies? How can you open the lines of communication on this subject and resolve any differences?

_____

_____

● What traditions and family activities do you look forward to sharing with your children?

> **Take Action!**
> Write a letter to your children sharing your hopes and dreams for them. Put it aside to show them when they graduate from high school. This will be a wonderful keepsake to share with your children.

A Baby Will Take Your Relationship to a Whole New Level of Commitment

Once you have a family, you're more motivated than ever to make your relationship work. There's so much more at stake—not just your own happiness, but that of your children as well. When problems arise, parents don't throw in the towel so easily. Even troubled couples or those that don't plan to marry are now bonded together for the welfare of the baby. The consequences are greater if things don't work out, and so they go the extra mile to get through the rough spots. They are no longer just committed to each other, but to their family.

> *Marriage is not an ongoing celebration of celestial dimension. It's a lifelong process of down-to-earth hard work worth every drop of sweat it produces.*
>
> —Glen Van Ekeren

Although Steve and Anna had never seriously thought about divorce—and certainly they argued just as much as any couple—they became more determined than ever to work on their problems after having children. Suddenly, they had to stay together not only for their own happiness, but for their children's welfare, too. Steve and Anna realized that there was much more at stake now when conflicts arose. They were a family now, and it was important for them to work through their problems instead of sweeping them under the rug. With this in mind, Steve and Anna set aside a half hour a night after the kids went to bed to reconnect. They both put aside their to-do lists to spend this time just to be.

Questions for Discussion

🌸 Do you feel you have a stronger commitment to each other now that you share a child? How does this make you feel?

_____

_____

🌸 Is it important to you to stay together for the sake of your children's well-being? What are the benefits for a child of having two parents present?

_____

_____

🌸 Are you more willing to work on conflicts now for the sake of family harmony? How will you begin to do this?

_____

_____

Take Action!

Reflect on the reasons you married your partner in the first place. Why did you want to spend the rest of your life with this person? Why did you choose to make this very important commitment? Write down your reasons and share them with your partner.

From "My Husband/Wife and I" to "My Family": A Baby Makes a Family

What do you share with your partner that you share with nobody else? Your children. You are the only two people in the world who have the joy of being these children's parents—together. You are a family unit. You are their mommy and daddy—the two people they want to be with more than anyone else in the world. You are united in this very important role.

Likewise, Madeleine and Tristan forged a link between Steve and Anna that no one else shared. They were their parents, their mother and father, and nobody else could fill their shoes in Madeleine and Tristan's eyes. It was a bond that could never be broken between them. Steve and Anna had created these beautiful children together and would always share in this joy. It was a "forever link" between Steve and Anna, and one more reason to keep their marriage healthy.

Questions for Discussion

❀ Do you feel a special bond with each other now that you share a child?

_____

_____

❀ How does it feel to know that your children are made up of the best parts of both of you? Do you sometimes stare at your children together and marvel at their perfection?

_____

_____

❀ Why did you pick each other to have a child with? Why did you think your partner would make a good parent?

_____

_____

Take Action!

Do something to symbolize the bond between you. Buy matching coffee mugs with your children's names on them! Have cards printed that say, "The (your last name) Family." Have a family portrait taken and display it prominently in your home and office.

CONCLUSION

According to _Parenting_ magazine (February 2006), "Studies show that the quality of the parents' marriage affects even very young babies in profound ways." That's why it's so very important to deal with "couple" issues early, before they escalate. By being aware of the challenges that arise when a baby (or two!) enters the household, and by focusing on the blessings that are also bestowed on a couple, a marriage can survive—and even thrive—in the first year of parenthood. Will there be tough times? You bet! Will your marriage experience some strain? Absolutely! Will you ever be tempted to boot your spouse out the door when the going gets rough? Most likely. (And he or she may be thinking the same thing!)

Raising a child is all-consuming, no doubt about it. But it is also the most important of the life experiences we live. Your marriage will be tested as never before! But together, you'll also experience more beautiful

When my wife and I got into fights before, sometimes I'd fantasize about walking out the door and living the single life again. Now that we have our sons, that thought has never even crossed my mind. I love my family and can't imagine life without them. Now when my wife and I disagree, I go the extra mile to work things out. I'll do whatever it takes to keep my family together.

—Jack Parker, father of a one- and three-year-old

moments than ever. After a while, you'll find that the "things" and the "stuff" that you miss are way down on the scale of importance compared to the new joys and experiences you'll embark on together. Like Steve and Anna, if you focus on the big picture and overlook the small stuff—if you redirect your efforts to forging a new relationship after the baby is born—you'll find that becoming parents is the best thing that ever happened to your marriage.

I'm really amazed at what a wonderful father my husband is. Seeing the gentle way he handles our daughter makes me love him even more. I can't believe we created this beautiful baby together.

—Ronnie Roberts, new mother

Four

Making a Living and Raising a Child: A Baby Will Change Your Views— and Goals—on Both

> You'll never "have it all." When you work, you're going to miss out on times with your children, and when you're home, you're missing out on career opportunities. It's part and parcel of the price you pay for the honor of being a parent.

Can you have a successful career and still be an involved parent? Will you be able to balance all of the responsibilities that go along with making a living and raising a child? Do you and your partner agree on your choices regarding work and parenting? Can you afford to stay home or to hire daycare if you work? So many questions arise when you find out you're pregnant. And these are scary questions that affect every aspect of your life: your finances, your marriage, your hopes and dreams, your child's well-being, your sense of self. You have some big decisions to consider about the changes you'll need to make in your life in order to take care of your baby, especially in the first year of her life. Most of the time, it's a matter of balance. Sure, before the baby, you had to work out a way to meet your obligations to your employers and clients, your spouse, and your household while making enough money to support yourselves. But now with the many demands of a baby's first year, the stakes seem so much higher!

We wanted to find out how today's parents are making these decisions and most of all if they are pleased with their choices, so we conducted some informal surveys. You'll see many of the results as you read this chapter. Think of them as advice from parents who have been where you are now—considering their options and doing what's best for their new family. We think you'll find their answers very helpful in your own life.

When [my daughter] started walking, I almost missed it. I am consumed with guilt because I'm a working mother. If I'm away for four hours I feel horrible . . . [but] my mother was never home. We turned out okay! . . . My mother's been there anytime I've needed her. That's really the message at the end of the day: I'm gonna be there for my daughter anytime she needs me.

—Leah Remini

And let's take a look at how another couple—Lawrence and Tawnee —handled the career and work issues that arose when they welcomed little Noell into the world.

At the age of thirty-three, Tawnee wasn't expecting that double-pink line to show up on the pregnancy test strip. She was proud of being the first African-American woman to rise to the position of dean of the engineering department at the university where she worked, and she and Lawrence hadn't planned on having children for a few more years yet. So she was quite shocked to find that she was pregnant. Lawrence couldn't have been more thrilled about the news, and reassured his wife that it would all work out. But Tawnee wasn't so sure. She feared the impact that her pregnancy and motherhood would have on her career—one that she had worked long and hard to achieve. But she had also read a lot of studies indicating that it was beneficial for children to have a parent at home. There was a daycare center for employees' children at the university, but somehow Tawnee just couldn't see herself leaving her child there all day—at least not for the first year.

Lawrence, on the other hand, was really excited about the pregnancy. He had always loved kids, and as the eldest child in his family, he had helped his parents out a lot with his younger siblings. In fact, he felt more confident about parenting than Tawnee did, who was an only child born to her parents late in life. As Tawnee's pregnancy progressed, she agonized over the decisions they would need to make. Should she give up her coveted position at work, one she dearly loved and that paid more than her husband's? Could they survive on Lawrence's income? Or should she continue to work and be uneasy knowing that her child was in daycare all day long? She just couldn't decide.

Lawrence, meanwhile, was beginning to give thought to another option. As a newspaper writer, he had access to a great deal of information, and he began to research the choices that other new parents had made. One particular article caught his eye. It discussed the rise in the number of stay-at-home dads. More and more fathers, the article said, were choosing to stay home with the children while the mothers returned to work. This was often the case if the mother's job paid more or the father had a position that could more easily be conducted from home. In Lawrence's case, both options applied. They really needed Tawnee's income, and Lawrence could easily do his research and writing from his computer at home—assuming he could convince his employer of his productivity. If time allowed, he could also pursue freelance jobs or start to tinker on the book he'd been itching to write. The more he thought about it, the more the idea grew on him. After receiving the okay from his boss, he broached the subject to Tawnee.

Tawnee had to admit that Lawrence's idea hadn't crossed her mind. She had just assumed that if one of them became a stay-at-home parent that it would be her. But the more she thought about it, the more the idea grew on her. It made financial sense and would be good for both their positions. She trusted that Lawrence could take care of the baby just as well as she could, and she knew that he would make a wonderful daddy. He was even great about working around the house, and he assured her that he could take on some of the laundry and cooking responsibilities. By the time baby Noell was born, they had made their decision. After an eight-week maternity leave for Tawnee, Lawrence would begin his "new job."

SIX WAYS A BABY WILL COMPLICATE
YOUR WORKING LIFE

Unless you've got a great nest egg and live-in help, having a baby is going turn your work world upside down. When you get married, you're supporting a household of two, and when a baby arrives, there are even more expenses. But you're also less available now to earn a paycheck. You feel like you're caught up in a Catch-22: If you devote yourself full time to your baby, you'll need to find alternatives to make up for the lost income. And if you return to a full-time job, you'll need to find ways to spend quality time with your baby. It involves a lot of painful choices for most couples. Let's take a look at some of the situations that arise career-wise when a baby enters the picture. Then we'll examine the ways becoming a parent can actually benefit your working life!

Your Time Will No Longer Be Your Own

It's a hard reality: You're expected to be on the job every working day, with very few exceptions. Those people who are always at the office doing their jobs well are usually the ones rewarded with promotions and raises. But if you find you're taking off a lot of time to tend to your family, your employer might not see you as being committed to the company or a team player. In short, you'll find it harder to climb the corporate ladder when you're not available to the company 24/7. The women in our survey also cited the fatigue factor: They were so tired from meeting the demands of their jobs as well as the needs of their families that they couldn't imagine working any harder at the office to get ahead. They were just too tired to do more than what was required on the job. To go above and beyond the call of duty to impress the boss no longer seemed feasible.

> *Of course, there are advantages to having your kids later—you can establish your career, and maybe you're more mature.*
>
> —Patricia Heaton

When Tawnee and Lawrence were considering their options, Tawnee was concerned that if her baby were placed in daycare, she wouldn't have the time to devote to her career. Many of her working friends' kids were always catching colds from the other children in their daycare centers, and their parents were constantly using up sick time to stay home with them or take them to the doctor. Also, daycare centers were very strict about the hours they maintained. What if a meeting ran late and she couldn't get to the daycare center before it closed? If she couldn't reach Lawrence to pick up the baby, it could be a real problem. And if her superiors noticed that she was neglecting her work to care for the baby, they might think twice about offering her any more career opportunities.

Questions for Discussion

❀ Were you career oriented before you had your baby? Do you think you're still as ambitious now that you have a child?

_____

_____

❀ Do you worry that you won't be able to work as efficiently— whether you work outside or inside the home—now that you have family responsibilities?

_____

_____

❀ Do you feel guilty when you have to take time from work to attend to a sick child or make up for a lapse in daycare?

_____

_____

❀ Do you think it's more difficult to climb the corporate ladder when you have small children?

_____

_____

❀ Do you have a strategy for maintaining your career? What are some of your options?

_____

_____

> ### Take Action!
>
> If advancing in your job is still a goal for you, it can be done, but extra planning is crucial. Try to find daycare that allows for flexibility, such as a small facility in a home setting or someone who comes to your home. Our survey participants preferred this option over a large daycare center. Also, plan ahead for backup care if needed. Is there a stay-at-home mother in the neighborhood who wouldn't mind a little extra cash to help out in a pinch? Perhaps baby's grandparents are close enough to help out now and then. Of course, if your child has more than a cold, you still may feel better staying home with her, but perhaps you can take home some work to do while she is napping. Keep your employer informed about what's going on, how you expect to get the work done, and when you think you'll be returning to work. They'll be impressed by your loyalty to the company despite your personal circumstances.

Lawrence and Tawnee's solution—to have Lawrence stay home with Noell—took care of many of the concerns that Tawnee cited. Because Noell was not in daycare, there were no time constraints on the hours that Tawnee could work. And if the baby had to go to the doctor or was ill, Lawrence was still available to care for her. Tawnee didn't have to use up her sick days if Noell had a cold. It's true that Tawnee missed being with Noell and probably spent a lot of time on the phone checking in with Lawrence, but overall she was able to focus on her career goals, knowing that Noell was in good hands.

You'll Miss the "Atta-Boys/-Girls"

Before you had a child of your own, how many times did you roll your eyes at the coworker who seemed to take off every other day to tend to a sick kid or attend a school function, or who lacked childcare for a working holiday? You had a hard time respecting this person when you were on the job every day, often picking up the slack for her being gone. You might even have felt resentful, especially if any of her job responsibilities fell to you. But the first time your babysitter cancelled and you had to stay home, you suddenly realized the conflicts that arise when you have responsibility for a child. Did you worry that you would now be the one losing your coworkers' accolades and respect? When we asked working mothers how family-friendly their workplace is, they told us, "Everyone talks a good game until you leave for the second time . . . or more." They definitely felt a lot of pressure to stay on the job even though their child was sick or they wanted to chaperone a school field trip.

> *The phrase "working mother" is redundant.*
>
> —Jane Sellman

Tawnee feared that she wouldn't look very professional if she were often out of the office attending to a baby's needs. She worked in a very formal office where business was taken very seriously. As a woman and a minority member, Tawnee felt especially pressured to prove herself on the job—to show that she didn't need any special privileges. Being respected for her accomplishments was important to Tawnee and she worried that she would lose some of the respect she'd worked so hard to attain if she was suddenly less visible on the job. And she wondered how she'd feel about herself: She had pursued her education—and this job. How could she sign out on all of that?

Questions for Discussion

❀ Have you ever been critical of someone at work who took off a lot of time to tend to sick children or attend school functions?

_____

_____

❀ If you're a working parent, are you concerned that your coworkers and superiors will resent any time off you take to care for a child?

_____

_____

87

❧ Do you think you'll be seen as less entitled to promotions if your job is no longer your highest priority?

_____

_____

> ### Take Action!
>
> Courtesy to your coworkers is key. Most people are understanding if you explain the situation and don't expect them to always make up for your absence. Communicate with those who work most closely with you: "Jeanie, I need to take the baby to the pediatrician this afternoon, but I plan to work on that proposal tonight and will have it on your desk first thing in the morning." Let people know you have things covered and they will respect you for not dropping everything on them or failing to let them know your Plan B.

Lawrence and Tawnee's arrangement meant that Tawnee had to spend little time away from the office, but she still felt bad that Lawrence was always the one to soothe Noell's feverish brow or attend baby massage classes with her. Tawnee vowed that if her daughter had a big problem, such as the time she got a severe ear infection, Noell wouldn't feel that her mother was neglecting her. She decided that sick days were available for a reason, and she was certainly going to use them if her child needed her! She knew that her absences were necessary and therefore she chose not to let her coworkers' resentment bother her. But at the same time, she made sure to always let them know how things would get done while she was gone. Tawnee felt less conflicted when she knew that both her baby's and her coworkers' needs were being met.

> _Don't sacrifice your life to make a living._
>
> —Lori Giovannoni

Finding Balance Will Be Tough—and Maybe Impossible

When you're working at a job—whether outside or inside the home—and meeting the demands of a family, it feels like something

88

always has to give. You can't devote 100 percent to everything. It's a tricky balancing act. Most of the women in our survey felt that finding balance was so difficult that they would stay home with their children full-time until their children started school if money weren't an issue—and if they felt they could step back into their career at some point. Single parents, of course, rued the fact that this wasn't even an option. Married women also felt there was an imbalance in the amount of responsibilities that both spouses assumed around the house. Things would be more equitable, they agreed, if their husbands lent more of a helping hand with household chores and errands. Men, on the other hand, said they would gladly come home if they felt they could still make the money they were making, and would help out more if their wives were less critical of the way they did things.

Because Tawnee's career consumed a lot of her time and energy, the last thing she felt like doing when she got home was making dinner and cleaning the house. But Lawrence also had a long day balancing his freelance career with caring for Noell, so he wasn't exactly excited about handling all of those responsibilities either. At first, they assumed that since Lawrence was home all day that he could take charge of the jobs around the house, but Lawrence soon realized that taking care of Noell and writing articles was already a full-time job. Clearly, he and Tawnee needed to work out different ways of getting things done around the house.

> *I have yet to hear a man ask for advice on how to combine marriage and a career.*
>
> —Gloria Steinem

Questions for Discussion

❀ Do you feel like you're constantly teetering back and forth between what needs to be done at work and what needs to be done around the house?

_____

_____

❀ Have you and your partner discussed how responsibilities will be handled so there is no resentment?

_____

● Do you think you've lost ground in keeping up with your household or work responsibilities since having a baby?

_____

_____

● Are there some duties that you can comfortably give up or modify to relieve the workload?

_____

_____

Take Action!

The next time you're feeling really stressed about getting something done, take a realistic look at it. Will the world end tomorrow if the floor isn't swept every single day? Will your family suffer if you bring home take-out once in a while instead of cooking a big meal? It's time to put things in perspective. Don't allow yourself to get stressed out by your to-do list. Sure, it would be great to have all the windows washed, but it would be even better to take your child to the park and play with her. Perhaps you can hire a neighborhood teenager to wash the car or mow the grass. Now is not the time to get hung up on perfection. Your children will only be young for a short time. Let a few things go and enjoy your children!

Lawrence and Tawnee decided to nip any resentment in the bud by clearly delineating each spouse's responsibilities for the household. They split up cooking nights and agreed that Fridays were phone-order pizza nights and Saturdays were for eating leftovers. On Sundays, they always went to Lawrence's parents' house for dinner, so that left just two days each week that they both had to cook. On Tawnee's cooking days, Lawrence was more than willing to help out by defrosting the meat or preheating the oven. They shopped for groceries together on Sundays after church. Lawrence did the laundry because it was easy enough for him to fit it around his other obligations, but Tawnee ironed the clothes since most of them were her working clothes anyway. Lawrence ran the errands that he could accomplish while taking Noell along, and Tawnee tackled those that were close to her office that she could do on her lunch hour. They split their other jobs down the middle. Because they agreed on what needed to be done, they didn't let any resentment build up over one taking on more responsibilities than the other.

> *A career is all very well, but no one lives by work alone.*
>
> —Lorna Luft

You're Going to Need (Good) Help

When both spouses have careers that aren't family-friendly, sometimes a change is in order. One parent may choose to leave his or her job altogether or go into a related occupation that can be done from home. Our survey participants frequently pursued real estate or computer careers that could be conducted out of a home office. Other times, one parent may choose to take a job that's not as enjoyable but that pays better in order to meet the expenses of a growing family. No longer do you have the luxury of just doing whatever work you wish. Sometimes sacrifices and changes need to be made for the good of the family.

Because Lawrence and Tawnee felt that daycare wasn't an option, one of them was forced to make a change. It wasn't possible for Tawnee to do her job from home. As a university dean, she was expected to be on campus full time, to be available to staff and students, and to attend various meetings and functions that were critical to the operation of the university. There was no way this could be a part-time position. Therefore, they had to consider a different situation.

Questions for Discussion

❀ Did you or your spouse make a career change when you had a baby? What were your reasons?

_____

_____

❀ Do you feel pressure to find a job that pays the bills and provides insurance rather than one that you enjoy more?

_____

_____

❀ Do you feel stuck in a particular job because you need to meet the financial needs of your family?

_____

_____

❀ Have you and your partner discussed ways in which you could change careers and still provide for the family?

_____

_____

Take Action!

If you'd like to pursue the option of working from home, at least part-time, the key is to make a great presentation to your employers. Don't just barge into your boss's office and say, "I want you to let me work from home." You need to draw up a plan showing how you will continue to meet the demands of your job when you're no longer in the office every day. Will you have a computer with high-speed Internet access and a fax line? Will you be available for conference calls with coworkers or the weekly company meeting? Ask other employees who work from home how they have made it work. Be aware that if your company has never allowed anyone to work from home, it might be a tough sell. Or you may need to be willing to assume a different position that is more conducive to working at home. Sell yourself and your proposal . . . and then don't let your employer down. Make sure you follow through on your promises so that you will continue to be allowed to work from home.

Unlike Tawnee, Lawrence's position as a newspaper writer was not supervisory. Because it was a relatively solitary job, he could easily work at a home office. Thanks to modern technology, he could research, write, and transmit stories through his computer and fax machine. Although it meant a drop in the family's income, they believed that the sacrifice was worthwhile in order for one parent to be with the baby all day. At one point, Lawrence was offered a full-time position by a large newspaper in another city. Although he might have jumped at the chance several years ago (before Tawnee's promotion), he knew that now was not the time. He and Tawnee had agreed that she would focus on her career and that it was important for Lawrence to be home with Noell. They agreed agreed that these changes were best for their family.

There's a Good Chance You'll
Need to Redo the Budget

As we alluded to above, expenses rise with each child, and this may affect your career choice. You may need to seek a job that pays more or offers better benefits, even if you don't like it as much. (This is especially true for single parents.) Let's face it, if we all waited until we felt financially prepared to have a child, we would never have children! Nevertheless, most new parents are shocked at the cost of baby supplies such as diapers and formula, and wonder how they will ever afford the expense of daycare. And how will they pay for additional health insurance, life insurance, and a college fund? This involves a lot of sacrifice, maybe even giving up on such goals as a new home or car for a while until finances get back under control. When we asked the stay-at-home parents in our survey if they ever felt financially pressured to return to work, they answered, "Money is always an issue." The good news is, starting a family really forces couples to take a hard look at their financial situation and make wise adjustments that will benefit their future.

> *It definitely puts a strain on family life—I miss them [the children] like mad. Being a working mother I've been juggling house and career from day one.*
>
> —Louise Jameson

Lawrence and Tawnee definitely felt the financial pinch when Lawrence quit his job. Although he continued to work from home, his income was drastically reduced from his full-time salary. And he was often engaged in writing his book, which would pay nothing until he could sell it to a publisher. And there was another factor he hadn't considered: Noell didn't sleep all day long. Caring for her, especially as she got older, Lawrence wasn't free to work as much as he'd anticipated. He would be halfway into a project and the baby would cry and need attention, or require feeding or changing. At one year of age, she took two naps, but when she was awake she wanted Daddy in her sight all the time. As Lawrence found out, working from home was not simply a matter of changing the location of his office. Caring for a child was, in many respects, a full-time job, so he was not as productive workwise as he thought he would be!

Questions for Discussion

❀ Are financial issues a greater concern now that you have a child? Are they a source of strain between you and your spouse?

_____
_____
_____
_____

> _Studies have shown that disagreements over money are the Number One cause of friction in a marriage. And for some, they're the Number One reason for divorce. . . . The key to success is to find the common ground—the shared values about how, as partners, you want to live your lives together._
>
> —Tawnee Bartiromo

❀ Do you worry about making ends meet with a family?

_____
_____

❀ Did you or your partner take a reduction in income in order to stay home or take a job that allowed you more flexibility to tend to your family?

_____
_____

❀ Were you surprised at the cost of baby supplies, health insurance, and other necessities when you had a child?

_____
_____
_____

> **Take Action!**
>
> A budget is essential. Look at all of your sources of income, then total all of your expenses. Are you seeing a deficit? Are you barely making it? When couples do this exercise, most are shocked at how much money is going out the door! Clearly, some revisions are in order. Perhaps you need to get quotes for less expensive insurance or downgrade your TV and Internet services. Are there more economical ways to meet your needs for food and other staples? Have you been treating yourself to little luxuries, like a pedicure or a daily Starbucks, which you can give up for a few years? If you're still having difficulties, a meeting with a financial planner or credit counselor may be in order. Take charge of your finances now before you get too deeply into debt.

On my second child's first birthday, it dawned on me that Ed McMahon and the Publisher's Clearinghouse money van were not going to be pulling up to my house any time soon . . . and that I'd better get a job if I was ever going to afford putting these kids through college.

—Molly Thomas, mom to Shannon, 3, and Brady, 1

Clearly, a new budget was in order for Lawrence and Tawnee. She started taking her lunch to work a couple of days a week instead of always going to the campus cafeteria or local restaurants. She cut down on buying work clothes and often shopped at outlet stores. She used the car that got the most economical gas mileage since she did more driving than Lawrence. They got a membership at a grocery warehouse to save money on food and baby supplies. Even though Tawnee was the primary breadwinner, they made all of their major financial decisions together so there was no resentment about unnecessary expenses.

Not Home Alone: You'll Feel Like You're "Not Working . . . Just Home with the Kids"

Issues of self-esteem often come into play when parents decide to stay home with the children. No longer are they an "accountant" or a "teacher" or "the boss"; now they're just Mom or Dad, which doesn't sound quite as impressive! If someone has asked you what you do, have you felt sheepish about saying you were a stay-at-home parent? Some people make up for this by saying, "Well, I'm trained as a nurse, but I'm taking a few years off to raise my children," as if they're ashamed that just being a parent is not impressive enough or their work is not as valuable as other work. Sometimes it's the working partner who makes you feel inferior. Our survey participants told us that if the working spouse had a bad day at the office, he or she would sometimes come home and make comments like "It must be nice not to work," or not be sympathetic to the stay-at-home parent's sources of stress.

> *The value of money is based on your own exchange rate.*
>
> —Lori Giovannoni

At first, Lawrence felt a little embarrassed telling people that he was a "stay-at-home dad." Some people, he assumed, would think he was less manly for taking care of a child full-time and allowing his wife to be the primary breadwinner. He had read in his research that it could sometimes be a little rough on the male ego, and he could understand why.

Questions for Discussion

● Do you think that a stay-at-home parent is doing work that is as valuable as that of, say, a corporate executive? Why or why not?

_____

_____

● If you're a stay-at-home parent, have you ever been embarrassed to admit this to people or have you quickly told them what you used to do before you quit your job?

_____

_____

❀ If you work outside the home, do you think that stay-at-home parents have it easy in terms of their responsibilities compared to yours?

_____

_____

> ### Take Action!
>
> If one of you is a stay-at-home parent, be proud of this new role! Raising a child is a very honorable and joyous profession. If you're the one who goes to the office, help your partner feel just as valuable by praising his or her accomplishments with the children. Don't be possessive about money just because you're the one who's bringing it in. Support each other in both your careers, and remember that the ultimate goal of this arrangement is to raise healthy, happy children. When we asked parents in our survey how they thought their children were doing as a result of their decision to have a parent at home, they answered, "The children are thriving!" Most wouldn't consider returning to the workplace until the children were teenagers or gone from home.

Lawrence realized that the issue of his worth was in his own head—and that he could, and would, tell himself the importance of upping the worth he assigned to it. He knew that his job taking care of Noell was a privilege for him and of equal importance to any other job that took place in an office. And by pursuing a writing career at home, Lawrence was still contributing to the family's finances and nurturing his career. As Lawrence gained more confidence in the value of his new role, he proudly announced to everyone that he stayed home with Noell all day. Being "Noell's daddy" was the most important job of his life right now. He knew this window to care for her wouldn't last forever and so he would cherish it while he could!

FOUR WAYS A BABY WILL ENHANCE YOUR WORK LIFE

While conflicts can certainly arise between your obligations to your job and your family, parenting can also be a benefit when it comes to making a living. For example, although it may force a job change, you may find that you actually like your new job better! Or you may find yourself having less stress on the job if you've decided to let go of your need to climb the corporate ladder for now to focus on your family. Raising children can also force you to take an honest look at your work and the time you spend doing it. It can cause you to search your values and define the meaning of success by your own standards.

> *The wealth of man is the number of things which he loves and blesses, which he is loved and blessed by.*
>
> —Thomas Carlyle

You'll Find That Having a Family Is Very Motivating!

Now that you have a family to support, you can no longer be a slacker. With your new grown-up role of being a parent comes the need to be more mature at the office. If you avoided applying for a management job in the past because you didn't want the headaches that came with it, you may be more willing to seek out that job now because it comes with a large increase in pay. The dads in our survey were especially of this mindset. They told us, "After I became a father, I invested more time at work, making sure the company saw me as promotable. I worked extra hard at making a good impression and did some projects or assignments I wouldn't have done previously when I wasn't supporting a child." Single mothers, as heads of the household, are also motivated to make more money.

Although Tawnee had always been a motivated worker, she became even more determined to excel now that her larger paycheck was supporting three people. Lawrence had taken a drop in pay since he was now working as a freelancer instead of receiving a salary, so Tawnee's income was the only one they could rely on. As the primary breadwinner, she now had greater motivation to be successful in her position—which was highly prized and well rewarded in the workplace.

Questions for Discussion

❀ In what way do you feel more motivated now to achieve career success so that you can better support your family?

_____

_____

❀ Do you feel more grown-up as a parent, and has this attitude carried over into the workplace?

_____

_____

❀ Does the thought of losing your job scare you more now that you have a family to support?

_____

_____

Take Action!

Being a parent gives us courage because we want to succeed for the sake of our family. So take a risk and seek that new position! Get up the nerve to ask for a raise. Give yourself (or your partner, if he or she is "going for it") a pep talk. Aim high. Brainstorm ways you can achieve your career goals. Think about how proud you'll feel when you hear your child say, "My daddy (or mommy) is the boss!"

You May Very Well Be a Better Manager

Now that you have a family of your own, you have more compassion for your coworkers' and subordinates' family concerns. After all, how can you be upset with the employee who takes a week off to be with her son during a bout with tonsillitis when your own child came down with the flu and was sick for several days? Now you understand the conflicts that other parents face. This is especially true for single parents, who don't have a partner to rely on when the kids get sick. And other parenting skills come in handy at the office as well. Our survey participants felt they were more focused on the job as the result of being a parent. They weren't willing to put up with "trivial stuff or time-wasting activities" because they just didn't want to be spending their valuable time dealing with unimportant things.

Tawnee admits that she was sometimes a little rough on colleagues who often missed work due to family obligations. But when Noell had a bout with pneumonia and was hospitalized, Tawnee had a better understanding of how parents can feel torn between the obligations of their jobs and the needs of their families. There was no way she would not be there for Noell during her illness, even though Lawrence was available to care for her. When Tawnee had to explain to her boss that she needed some time off, she realized the difficulty that her own subordinates must have faced in asking her for leave time to attend to family needs. She resolved to be more understanding of their situations in the future, and she looked for ways to help her staff develop better skills—such as job sharing and sabbaticals—to handle the stresses, strains, and pressures of the job. In short, she better understood the skillset needed to balance the responsibilities of parenting and career—and allow neither to suffer.

> *Your outlook upon life, your estimate of yourself, your estimate of your value are largely colored by your environment. Your whole career will be modified, shaped, molded by your surroundings, by the character of the people with whom you come in contact every day.*
>
> —Orison Swett Marden

Questions for Discussion

❁ In what ways has becoming a parent made you more understanding of others?

_____

_____

❁ Do you ever feel guilty when the needs of your child conflict with your work obligations?

_____

_____

❁ What parenting skills do you find to be beneficial at the

office?

_____

_____

❁ What parenting concerns have made you less available on the job?

_____

_____

Take Action!

The next time someone at work has to leave to attend to a sick child, imagine how you'd feel in his or her place. Wouldn't it be lovely if your coworkers showed some concern for your child's welfare or offered to take some of the workload off your plate? Start a new company "compassion trend." When an employee returns, ask how her child is doing. And let her know that you covered for her when she was out for a third day and the vice president came looking for her. You can be sure that the next time you can't be around, your grateful coworker will show you the same compassion.

You'll Have "New and Improved" Priorities

You'll be amazed at how your career priorities change when you have a child. Pre-baby, you may have been willing to do anything possible to move ahead at the office. It didn't matter if you were working nights and weekends because you were moving up. But now the big picture has changed. Although it's still important to do a good job, you realize that rising to the top isn't necessarily what you want anymore. You're not willing to give up your life at the expense of your children's well-being. This can free you up from the stress of your formerly competitive life and allow you to be more content with your current status in life.

Although Tawnee still felt a desire to continue to progress in her career, she felt more balanced about her ambitions when she became a mother. Noell's well-being would always be the ultimate test of whether a business decision would be right for her. Before having the baby, she would have accepted almost any position that offered more money and prestige. But now she knew that if it would be detrimental to her relationship with Noell in any way—for instance, if it involved a great deal of travel—that she would turn it down. Noell now came first, no matter what.

Questions for Discussion

❀ Do you feel more or less driven in your career now that you have a child?

_____

_____

❀ Do you have the same career goals that you did before you had children?

_____

_____

❀ Do you see a conflict between raising children and rising to the top at work?

_____

_____

❀ In what ways are you more balanced? Has anyone noticed?

_____

_____

> **Take Action!**
>
> It's important to have career goals, but sometimes they just need to be broader. If you've become a stay-at-home parent, perhaps your new goal is to find a job once your child starts school. Start thinking now about what you'd like to do and how to prepare for it, perhaps through volunteer work, working from home, or taking classes. If you want a management position at work, better timing might be to plan for a few years down the road when your children aren't so needy. You don't have to give up your dreams; just know that the timing may need to change. Usually, if you have something to look forward to or a plan for achieving it, you won't feel as if your current sacrifices are painful.

You'll Bring a Deeper Sense of Self to Your Work (and Goals)

Changing jobs or career paths can be scary. If you decide the time is right to pursue a freelance job at home, you may worry that you won't be able to pick up enough work to keep afloat financially. Or you may feel that you'll be bored or too distracted by the demands of home and children to do your job properly. If you change jobs but still work outside the home, there are the usual anxieties of hoping that you'll like the new job, that you'll get along with your new coworkers and boss, and that you won't be looked down upon if you need to take time off for a sick child. But often, being forced to change careers may turn out to be for the best. You may find a whole new career that you love, such as becoming a daycare provider or a children's book author. Or perhaps you'll find that your new job is much less stressful than your old one. At the least, time away will provide perspective.

Lawrence found that staying home with Noell was actually a boon to his career. Not being in an office, he was away from the distractions that often accompanied an office job—ringing phones, coworkers stopping by to chat, announcements over the PA system. The more peaceful environment at home was more conducive to writing—especially during her morning and afternoon nap times. And when Noell got older, Lawrence hired a sitter for two hours each day so he could use that time to return phone calls and write. Lawrence also found that his experiences with his daughter fueled him with ideas for writing, and so he found himself producing more creative work. He sold several articles on being a stay-at-home father and started to send out book proposals on the subject to publishers. In addition, as a parent, he now took a greater interest in issues that affected the safety of his community and world. This, too, gave him a passion for new writing topics. It worked out well for him.

> _I don't have a career plan. As I get older, different things become important to me. And frankly, I'm a dad, so it's like how long is it?_
>
> —Campbell Scott

Questions for Discussion

❀ Have you thought about pursuing a career that's more conducive to raising a child?

_____

_____

❀ If you did change jobs, are you happy with your decision? Why or why not?

_____

_____

❀ If you have more children in the future, will you need to revisit your decision to stay at home or return to work?

_____

_____

Take Action!

Be proactive. Many people stagnate in a job they dislike because they're afraid to make a change. Follow your heart. Perhaps now is the perfect time to try a new career or pursue one from home. You'll never get a better sign that the time is right than when you have a baby. Instead of complaining about how your job takes you away from home, strategize! Can you pursue a degree online or take weekend classes to become certified for work that gives you a more flexible job schedule? Can you get licensed as a daycare provider and watch other children so you can stay home with yours? Can your current job be conducted from home, even if it's only part-time? Look at all of your options and consider all opportunities. Create the life that you want.

CONCLUSION

Our survey participants all agreed that you'll never have it all. When you work, you're going to miss out on times with your child, and when you're home, you're missing out on money and career opportunities. It's a price you pay for the honor of being a parent. Most of all, you can't give 100 percent of your time to both your job and your children. Despite this seemingly gloomy insight, most parents in our survey felt their children were doing just fine, regardless of their career choices. Somehow, each family made the right decisions and managed to raise and support children to the best of its abilities. The key is preparation. Carefully consider your choices, along with the associated pros and cons, and then make the best decision for your family. We have confidence that your children will thrive on whatever path you choose!

Five

A Baby . . . Creates Family Ties— and Bonds That Bind

> The need to belong is hugely important to our emotional security. The family unit is the most basic building block in developing this important aspect of self: We are someone special to someone special! There is great security in that.

As we've examined in previous chapters, your relationships with your friends and spouse are greatly affected by a baby's arrival, but so are the ways in which you relate to others in your extended family. Let's say, for instance, that a parent-in-law has a subtle but sure way of making you feel you aren't necessarily the person she would have chosen to be her child's spouse. But now when you come around, holding that cute little grandchild, well, grandparent soon figures out a way to lose the attitude if she wants to find favor in your eyes and be granted time with the baby! And no doubt you'll also have to learn some diplomacy. Before the baby, you could keep your visits with the in-laws short but sweet. But you aren't the baby's only parent; your spouse will have some say in shaping the family dynamics as well. And there's the baby to think of: How can you deny your precious child the chance to know the grandparents or aunts and uncles and cousins—including a couple of them who feel obligated to comment on the way you do things?

Yes, once a baby arrives, it's suddenly a family affair. And, of course, this is as it should be. While coping with certain family members can be trying, nevertheless, as the old saying goes, blood is thicker than water. In other words, of all the relationships we court in life, those we trust and confide in most are often the favorites within our family. Certainly, the relationships between our children and their grandparents are among their most prized associations. And many times an aunt or uncle will have a profound and lasting influence on a child's life as well. Of course this also holds true of siblings, who after our parents create the deepest bonds for life—for good or bad. Whether in celebration or in times of mourning, the family unit is one of our most important sources of belonging.

But if family relationships are troubled, they may improve when a child enters the picture. Perhaps you never had much in common with your brother, but now that you're both parents, you find that you share more and more interests. Or maybe now you understand why your mother made certain decisions when you were young that you didn't agree with at the time. And if you have stepchildren, the addition of a half-sibling can either bring you closer together or drive a deeper wedge between you. Of course, every family situation is different, so we can't possibly cover all the bases as to how a baby will affect your particular family, but we can predict that it will impact the relationships you share with your extended family members in some way or another. Let's take a look at Nancy and Robert's story, as well as some of the more frequent situations that arise within families when babies are born.

Nancy and Robert were high school sweethearts and still lived in the same small town where they had grown up. Their parents and most of their siblings lived nearby. For the most part, Nancy and Robert liked it that way. Their families were always around to lend a hand or hang out with. When Nancy and Robert endured two years of fertility treatments, they found a lot of solace in their extended family. And when twins Adam and Amanda finally arrived, the whole family was over the moon. Everyone was thrilled that Nancy and Robert were finally parents, and couldn't get enough of the sight of their precious babies. All their relatives were a big help when the twins came home from the hospital. Robert's parents came for two weeks, and Nancy's parents followed. After that, it seemed like someone was always around or just a phone call away to lend a hand.

At first, it was great. But after a while, it got to be more of a nuisance. It seemed as if every time Nancy had just gotten the twins down for a nap, someone was calling or walking through the door, disturbing Nancy's only chance to do housework or rest. And the well-meaning advice! It was neverending! "You're going to stay home with the twins, right? All the Benson mothers have always been stay-at-home mothers." Or "The babies in this family have always been baptized at First Church of God. We know you go to that other church, but you can't break tradition by not having the baptism at First Church!" And while Nancy and Robert appreciated childrearing tips at first, it got to be too much after a while as relatives felt free to provide advice without being asked to.

But Nancy and Robert also realized how lucky they were that their children would have a chance to grow up within a large extended family and spend lots of time with grandparents, aunts and uncles, and cousins. They knew that many families today are spread all over the map, so they felt blessed that their children would be surrounded by a great deal of love. If only they could find that balance between being too far apart and too close!

FOUR WAYS A BABY WILL TEST AND CHALLENGE YOUR FAMILY TIES

From unwanted advice to increased obligations, sometimes our families can really test our patience. As that old saying goes, you can't pick your family, and naturally all families are made up of all types of people. With some family members, we get along fine; with others, well, let's just say we wish they'd stay on their own branch of the family tree. But as children enter the picture and we

Nobody has ever before asked the nuclear family to live all by itself in a box the way we do. With no relatives, no support, we've put it in an impossible situation.

—Margaret Mead

attach greater importance to being a family, it's necessary to examine the problems that can crop up and the best ways of dealing with them.

You'll Get (Overrated) Unsolicited Advice!

The greatest complaint we hear from new parents about their extended family relates to unwanted advice. Nobody likes a meddler. As Publilius Syrus said, "Many receive advice; few profit by it." Sure, we have plenty of insecurities about parenting and don't mind asking others for their wisdom, but when advice is unsolicited, it's a different story. First of all, it comes across as criticism—as though either we are not wise enough to figure out how to do something for our own baby, or that the way we wish to do it is not best or even right. Being made to feel dumb or inadequate is not good—even if the person giving the advice was crowned Mother-of-the-Year. If your mother-in-law says, "You would look so cute with short hair," you immediately assume that she finds something wrong with the way you wear your hair now. You were perfectly happy with the way your hair looked until your mother-in-law's comment threw you into doubt about your decision to grow out your hair.

The same thing can happen with decisions you make about your children. Say you've decided to discontinue breastfeeding after four months and your sister-in-law tells you, "I've heard that kids pick up illnesses a lot more when they're on formula. You should really keep trying to nurse." Your own doctor assured you that your decision was fine, and you resent your sister-in-law's comment; it still makes you feel inadequate, or worse, like a terrible parent. And the next time the baby gets sick, you'll be wondering if your sister-in-law was right! Nobody knows why relatives are prone to giving unsolicited advice. Siblings are especially vulnerable to this syndrome as they carry over their competitiveness from childhood. And in-laws may have a hard time accepting that you do things differently in your family than in theirs. But understanding the reasons behind their comments doesn't make them any easier to endure.

Robert's mother Phyllis had raised six children, so she certainly had a lot of experience in raising kids. Because she had such a large family, Phyllis was a more relaxed mother than Nancy. If Nancy fussed over whether the twins were dressed warmly enough for the weather, Phyllis would say, "Oh, just forget the jacket! I've got a blanket in the diaper bag if I feel it's necessary!" And when Phyllis babysat the twins, Nancy felt frustrated when she got home and found that Phyllis had let them play on the floor without first laying down a blanket. When she tried to discuss it with Phyllis, her mother-in-law would just say, "Oh, they'll be fine! I let all my kids play on the floor, and even though they ate a bug here and there, they survived it!" Although Robert sympathized with Nancy, he didn't want to cause friction with his mother, so he wouldn't speak up.

> *The greatest thing in family life is to take a hint when a hint is intended—and not to take a hint when a hint isn't intended.*
>
> —Richard Bach

Questions for Discussion

🌸 Do you find that your extended family is more involved in your lives now that you're parents? What do you think about that?

_____

_____

🌸 Do you have a family member who loves to offer unsolicited advice? How does it make you feel?

_____

_____

🌸 How do you handle advice that's not welcome? Do you confront the advice-giver or ignore it?

_____

_____

🌸 Does your spouse support any conflicts you have with your in-laws?

_____

_____

🌸 Has any advice from family members caused you to doubt your parenting style?

_____

> **Take Action!**
>
> We tend to be extra sensitive to relatives' advice. A close friend's counsel usually goes over better than that of a parent, sibling, or in-law. The next time you're the recipient of unwanted advice, consider whether you might be reacting negatively because of the source. Try to imagine the same advice coming from a friend. Don't assume that every suggestion is a criticism. Even if you're convinced you're not being overly sensitive, don't let your reactions harm your family relationships. Learn not to let things get under your skin. Not only will it improve your relationships, but it will also decrease the stress in your life and make you a healthier and happier person. And here's some advice that will help you hold your tongue the next time someone fires away: You are the parent—which means you're the boss!

Nancy knew that her mother-in-law wasn't intentionally trying to undermine her; Phyllis needed to feel needed and to know that her expertise was appreciated. As a full-time mother, she had made raising children her life's work, and it was the only thing that she really felt competent in. So Nancy made a point of starting to ask her mother-in-law for advice when she really did want it or knew she'd be willing to follow it. For instance, Phyllis was an excellent cook, so Nancy consulted her for ideas on what to serve at the twins' christening party. As Nancy made more of an effort to make Phyllis feel that her opinions mattered, she noticed that the number of unwanted suggestions went down. When one of them slipped out, Nancy learned to simply say, "I'll think about that, thanks" and continue with what she was doing.

Family Dynamics Will Change—and Not All Changes Will Be for the Better!

When you become a parent, you become a different person. As we've shown in other chapters, your priorities shift, you become more responsible, and your interests change. This can cause alienation within the family. For example, you may not have as much time to spend with a younger sister now that you're a mother. Or if you and your brother always went hunting every weekend of deer season, he may resent that you can only spare one weekend this year because your family needs you. The cousin who used to be your best date for the women's book club that the two of you belonged to may feel left out or abandoned now that you're no longer available to attend on a regular basis.

> *I haven't spoken to my mother-in-law for eighteen months. I don't like to interrupt her.*
>
> —Ken Dodd

Robert's older brother Tim was less than thrilled about the turn of events when Robert became a dad. Tim and his wife had no children—having made the choice to not have kids—and they had often gone out to dinner with Robert and Nancy. After the twins were first born, going out to dinner or a movie was out of the question. But even when going to an early dinner with the twins, Robert and Nancy still found it a strain to hang out with Tim and his wife, who weren't kid people and didn't like it when the twins cried or needed a bottle in the middle of dinner. And Tim and Laura could no longer bring their dog over to Robert and Nancy's house because the babies were allergic to it. The once close relationship between the two couples slowly but surely ground down, at least while the babies were young. When the twins matured a bit, perhaps they could build a new form of relationship. After all, said Tim, "I can't wait until the babies get older and we can take them along with us camping!"

Questions for Discussion

❀ Are you spending less time with certain family members than you did before your child was born? Why? Do you feel it will take a back seat for good, or just for now?

113

_____

_____

❀ How has having a child affected your interests, topics of conversation, or choices of activities?

_____

_____

❀ Is it possible to maintain relationships when the dynamics change, as they did with the couples above? How can this be done?

_____

_____

Take Action!

Is there someone in your family whom you've been neglecting since you became busy with the demands of parenting? Make an effort to call them or send them a card. You may need to accept that you won't have as many reasons to get together anymore, but most relationships are valuable and worth maintaining in some way. Make a point of not letting yourselves grow apart because your circumstances change. Keep in touch.

Although Robert and Nancy knew that nothing could be done to change the situation (Tim and Laura's decision to not have kids seemed permanent and, of course, the twins were there to stay!), they nevertheless missed the closeness that they had once shared. When the twins got older, Robert and Nancy made a point of hiring a sitter once a month so they could go to dinner with Tim and Laura without the children. They made every attempt not to talk too much about the children (although it was hard!) and to focus on other interests instead. It was clear that things had changed—Robert and Nancy could no longer discuss the latest movies, for example, because they never went to the theater—but they still felt it was worthwhile to maintain the relationship they'd always cherished. Hopefully, as the twins got closer to school age, Tim and Laura wouldn't feel so awkward around them and would interact with them more.

> *If you don't understand how a woman could both love her sister dearly and want to wring her neck at the same time, then you were probably an only child.*
>
> —Linda Sunshine

Your Obligations to Family Members Will Increase

As your parental responsibilities increase, so do your obligations to your family. Whereas before you became a parent you might have been able to avoid the family Thanksgiving dinner with the excuse of a ski trip, you're now expected to bring the baby and join in the family festivities. And how can you not spend Christmas with the grandparents? Of course, they'll want to watch the children open their gifts. Cousin Billy's confirmation? Your niece Molly's kindergarten graduation? You're definitely expected to make an appearance! Of course, you may love these activities and don't have a problem going to them, but you feel at least some pressure to do these things and believe that you no longer have the option to attend or not because you have kids of your own.

Just as you want your parents and siblings to be there for your child, so it is important that you be there for the others in your extended family. And then there are the conflicts between "his" and "her" families. Both sets of grandparents want to see the children on the holidays. As for you, you find it stressful to travel all day and would rather have a nice quiet day at home with your spouse and your own kids. You feel as if you'll never please everybody.

Robert and Nancy found this conflict happening more and more frequently. The year that Robert's godson's high-school graduation fell on the same day as Nancy's sister's wedding was especially stressful. Robert had been an important influence in Caleb's life, and had been in the bleachers at almost all of Caleb's soccer and football games. But Nancy's sister was having a big wedding with Nancy as the maid of honor! No question about it, Caleb and his parents would be disappointed if Robert weren't there. But of course they had to be at the wedding, no matter what.

Questions for Discussion

❀ Do you feel more of an obligation to attend family events now that you have children of your own?

_____

_____

❀ Do you enjoy family happenings more now that you have your own children?

_____

_____

❀ What are the benefits of attending family gatherings?

_____

_____

❀ How do you and your partner handle conflicts between "his" and "her" family events?

_____

_____

❀ After these occasions, do you feel satisfied with the family bonding that happened? Do you look at them as obligations, or do you feel that you are building important relationships?

_____

_____

Take Action!

Even though we sometimes accept family invitations with a feeling of dread, in the long run we realize how very important these get-togethers are for the sake of family bonding. When you focus on the positive goal of building family relationships, you'll come to see these gatherings as being beneficial rather than an obligation.

The wedding was out of town, so there was just no way that Robert and Nancy could attend his godson's graduation. But nonetheless, it was extremely important to them to be there in spirit for Caleb. They made sure to call Caleb on the day of his graduation, and they took him out to a very special dinner the week after they returned. Although they were disappointed at missing the graduation, Nancy and Robert were pleased to find some way to honor Caleb for his accomplishment.

> *Having a family is like having a bowling alley installed in your brain.*
>
> —Lyndon Baines Johnson

A Baby Is Sure to Be a Source of Sibling Rivalry

Most people rationalize having a second or third child by saying that they want to provide a playmate for their other children, so they're often surprised to find that their children aren't particularly grateful to add another chicky to the nest! The firstborn child may have grown accustomed to being the apple of her parents' eyes, so she doesn't appreciate being toppled from her throne by an adorable baby brother! Siblings often see each other as competition for their parents' affection or for any accomplishments they may achieve. They may become jealous if their brother shows signs of being a budding artist when they can't draw a straight line or if their sister catches a baseball better than they do. If stepchildren are involved, that also complicates the family dynamics. A stepdaughter may feel that her stepmother loves her "real" daughter more than her or that the baby gets more attention from her. It's true that many of us grow close to our siblings in adulthood, but in the meantime we can make things quite miserable for our parents when we don't get along. Interestingly enough, even pets can experience sibling rivalry when a baby enters the household! They may act up by refusing to eat or, in the case of cats, developing an aversion to the litter box.

> *When our relatives are at home, we have to think of all their good points or it would be impossible to endure them.*
>
> —George Bernard Shaw

117

Of course, Robert and Nancy never anticipated there would be sibling rivalry in their house. Because of their infertility, they weren't even sure they'd be able to have one child, let alone two. And though they were thrilled with their two-for-one deal, they found that as the twins got older and interacted more, they competed for the same toys and battled for their parents' affection. When Nancy was holding Adam on her lap, Amanda would push him off so that she could sit there. And even if there were a hundred toys to choose from, Adam and Amanda always seemed to want the same one. If one child had a particular toy, it was immediately attractive to the other twin. Robert and Nancy were also surprised to see how physical things got. The twins would bite and hit each other to get their way. This was a source of stress they had not anticipated when they envisioned having a child. In fact, they gained a new appreciation for what their own parents must have gone through when Robert and Nancy were children.

> *Children of the same family, the same blood, with the same first associations and habits, have some means of enjoyment in their power, which no subsequent connections can supply.*
>
> —Jane Austen, Mansfield Park, 1814

Questions for Discussion

❀ Did you experience sibling rivalry when you were growing up? How did your parents handle it?

_____

_____

❀ If you have more than one child, is there any resentment or competition between them? How does it make you feel? Do you handle it the same way as your parents did or differently?

_____

_____

❀ If you have more than one child, what were your reasons for expanding your family?

_____

_____

❀ If you have more than one child, did you anticipate sibling rivalry? If so, how did you think it would play out, and what did you say you'd do to help everyone adjust?

_____

_____

❀ Do you think your children will appreciate each other more when they get older? Do you appreciate your siblings more now that you're adults?

_____

_____

Take Action!

Curb sibling rivalry by making an effort to treat your children as individuals. Make sure to reserve private time alone with each child. Some families give each child a day of her own to call the shots on the activities for the day or to go out to lunch with a parent, not taking her sibling along. Never compare your kids to each other. Each has her own talents, strengths, and weaknesses. Learn to look for the good and praise it. Make each child feel special and cherished for herself.

Robert and Nancy joined a parents-of-twins group so they could gather input from other parents. They picked up some great tips from other parents of multiples, but even when their children didn't turn into instant angels, it helped Robert and Nancy just to know that their behavior was normal and every difficult stage they went through wouldn't last for long. They also read many books on parenting, especially of twins, and tried many techniques for curbing the sibling rivalry. Not all of them helped, but Robert and Nancy felt better knowing they were being proactive in nipping unacceptable behavior in the bud.

As a new grandparent, what struck me most about the birth of my grandchild was a profound feeling of HOPE. There was within me a complete shift of "renewal." Suddenly, I was needed in a way I'd never felt before. This feeling needed was not that I'd be useful as a sitter, or that now and then I'd give the parents a break from things. It was an unexpected bestowal of being granted the prestige of being a wiser "sage" in the family. There was this lovely feeling of, "I must be wise for this new family." For some reason, while I loved them and this new child, I stood taller, felt stronger, grew "wiser," and I knew these feelings to be good for my mental health and that I'd live longer—I had to. How could my precious grandbaby and her parents do or be without me? To grandparents, our grandchildren offer us a renewal that no "earthly" work or rose gardens can.

—a new grandmother

FOUR WAYS A BABY WILL ENHANCE AND ENRICH YOUR FAMILY TIES

While family relationships certainly get more complicated when children enter the fold, they can also be enriched as never before. Family celebrations become more important, and being there to honor and celebrate milestones of each family member can give you a sense of belonging. The outside world may or may not think of you as "The World's Best Mom" but chances are, there is a place in your family for such an honor and more. Even rifts can be mended as people realize they don't want to waste another minute being upset and away from their family members. With children comes healing. You now understand why your sister is so protective of her kids or why your mother wouldn't let you get your ears pierced or join the football team when you were seven. And having children affords more opportunities to spend time together. School, sporting, and church events are all occasions for the whole family to gather. The birth of a baby is a time of renewal for many families.

You'll Have a Family for Your Child

Most people crave family. This may be especially true if you didn't have close relationships with your extended family when you were growing up. People from families that weren't close often seem to marry someone from close-knit families because it provides the togetherness they long for. And when we have our own children, we want them to benefit from the whole family experience, surrounded by the company and love of relatives. Family traditions are also treasured. As troublesome as they can sometimes be, as we discussed previously, at the same time we know our lives would be very empty without family in them—and we don't want that to happen to our children.

As much as their families sometimes got on their nerves, Robert and Nancy were still happy that they lived in an area that was close to their relatives. They had fond memories of growing up with lots of siblings and cousins around, and they hoped to give Adam and Amanda the same experience they had. They took comfort in knowing that if something happened to them, there would always be family around to care for and love the twins. It was comforting to be wrapped in the arms of their family.

> *The lack of emotional security of our American young people is due, I believe, to their isolation from the larger family unit. No two people—no mere father and mother—as I have often said, are enough to provide emotional security for a child. He needs to feel himself one in a world of kinfolk, persons of variety in age and temperament, and yet allied to himself by an indissoluble bond which he cannot break if he could, for nature has welded him into it before he was born.*
>
> —Pearl S. Buck

Questions for Discussion

❀ When you were a child, did you spend a lot of time with extended family members or not?

_____

_____

❀ What kind of family would you like your own child to have?

_____

_____

121

🌸 How can you ensure that your child gets to know more of your family?

_____

_____

🌸 What are the benefits to a child of having a close extended family?

_____

_____

🌸 Does everyone in your family know each other—do you think each could draw a family tree?

_____

_____

Take Action!

Today, many families aren't as fortunate as Robert and Nancy to live close to their relatives. Cousins often grow up not knowing each other very well because they live so far apart. It's hard to find families who know everyone in the family tree. You can make up for this omission by creating your own family tree with as much of your extended family included as possible. (You may need to consult with Grandma or a great-aunt to get all the names!) Then mail a copy to all your baby's cousins with a special card. Even if they're too young to read it yet, it will be a precious keepsake for them as they grow. It's a wonderful way to show that even though you may live far away, you want the next generation of little ones to know—and claim!—each other.

You Can Count on Your Family to Be There for Your Child

Having family means your child is special to someone, and as such, accepted. She doesn't have to do too much to earn her place. She doesn't need to stop hitting her sister over the head with the toy before she gains love and affection. And she doesn't need to win the science fair or even get on the honor roll. Belonging to a family is automatic acceptance. And this is a very privileged place to be. Friends will come and go. People will frequently reject you, or prize their relationship with you only if it's good for them. But when you're part of a family, you're a piece of the family puzzle—and regardless of your size, shape, and disposition, you're one of the pieces, and there is a place just for you. Your children also become a piece of the puzzle and, as such, have a place in the world; they'll find security in that. Most likely you can count on your family, especially your parents, to shower your child with love. And who else will get all excited to get a handmade card from your child that says, "I love my auntie," or "Gamma, you're the greatest." It's a special feeling, to be sure. We are someone special to someone special!

Nancy and Robert knew that with such a big family around, their twins would never feel lonely or unwanted. It was a blessing for them to feel part of a family, to be privy to the family's inside jokes and traditions. Both sets of grandparents just adored the twins and had already started college funds for them. The twins' eyes would light up when "Pap-Pap" or "Mamaw" came to visit. Their cousins loved to go to Robert's sister's house and play with her five children—and they knew it was just a matter of time before Adam and Amanda would be a part of that family fun. It was a special feeling knowing that their families would continue through another generation.

Questions for Discussion

● Which family members are particularly close to your child?

_____

_____

● Do your children look forward to visits from others in your family?

_____

_____

● Does your family have any pet names for your child?

_____

_____

Take Action!

Make sure you and your partner have designated guardians for your child in case something happens to you. You can't necessarily assume that your child would go to a particular person. And before making it official, be sure to ask permission of your choice of guardian. It's a great way to ensure that they stay involved in your child's life and get to know and care for him or her.

Family is the first social unit for developing the qualities of the heart. A true family grows and moves through life together, inseparable in the heart. Whether a biological family or an extended family of people attracted to each other based on heart resonance and mutual support, the word "family" implies warmth, a place where the core feelings of the heart are nurtured. Family values represent the core values and guidelines that parents and family members hold in high regard for the well-being of the family. Sincere family feelings are core heart feelings. They are the basis for true family values. While we have differences, we remain "family" by virtue of our heart connection. Family provides necessary security and support, and acts as a buffer against external problems. A family made up of secure people generates a magnetic power that can get things done. They are the hope for real security in a stressful world.

—Sara Paddison, Hidden Power of the Heart

A Child Can Enrich, Even Mend, Relationships

Children have an innate talent for mending relationships. If you never really had much in common with your mother, the bond you now share with the birth of a child can give you reason to be together. Perhaps you and your sister never had a close relationship, but as your chil-

> *If you cannot get rid of the family skeleton, you may as well make it dance.*
>
> —Benjamin Franklin

dren love playing with her children, you find yourself getting together more often—and pushing aside old hurts. When your child asks, "Why are you mad at Uncle William?" and you can't even remember what the fight was about, you know it's time to mend fences. And getting the children together can be a good icebreaker for reestablishing a relationship.

Robert's relationship with his father-in-law had never been the best. Nancy's dad Frank seemed to resent Robert for taking away his "little girl"—especially since Robert had talked her out of joining her father in the family business. When Nancy and Robert broke up briefly to "spread their wings" before they got married, Frank blamed Robert for deserting Nancy, and even though Nancy had long since gotten over the temporary breakup, it seemed to Robert that her father still did not trust him. Things had never been the same between them, and they often avoided each other's company. With Adam and Amanda's arrival, Nancy's father was now over at the house more often. When Frank saw how devoted Robert was to Nancy and the kids and what a great father he was—even changing diapers, something that was never done in Frank's time—he began to see Robert with new eyes. Although Robert would never be as close to Frank as he was to his own father, they forged a new relationship based on their mutual love for Nancy and the twins. Robert was relieved to finally be approved as Frank's daughter's husband.

Questions for Discussion

❁ Are there any rifts in your family?

❀ Has the arrival of your child improved or worsened your family relationships?

❀ Are you spending more time with your in-laws now that you have a child? How do you feel about that?

❀ In what ways can a child be healing for a family?

Take Action!

If you've been distanced from someone in your family and want to make peace, take the initiative. There's nothing wrong with calling to say, "I'd like to bring the baby over to see you." There's no need to go into old hurts at this first visit. Just enjoy the time together with your baby and let your new relationship unfold gradually and naturally. Watching a child play provides material for some great conversations to avoid awkward silences.

A Child Can Give You More in Common with Family Members

When siblings have many years between them, they may find that they have little in common. For instance, if your brother is ten years older than you, he may have been married with children while you were still struggling with high school issues. Or perhaps you and your sister are close in age, but you always had entirely different interests. You went to college, eventually becoming a partner in a law firm, while your free-spirited sister drifted from one city to the next, seemingly content to never settle down. And so for many years you seemed to have little in common. But having children gives you a link. While you could never consult your sister about your lifestyle choices, you can now call and ask her how she survived her child's first day of preschool—or whether she thinks it's all that bad to take your child from one school in the middle of the school year to place him in a different school. You now share a connection.

Having both come from large families, Nancy and Robert were naturally closer to the siblings who were nearer to their own age. But now that they had kids of their own, they found themselves calling their older siblings more and more to get the benefit of their experience. Nancy had always felt that her oldest sister Susan had done a great job of raising her children, who had all gone on to college and successful lives, so she called Susan often to find out her secrets of success. Nancy and Robert were thrilled to finally forge new and better relationships with their older siblings. And Robert got to know his teenage sister better when she volunteered to babysit for the twins. She obviously adored being around the twins, and Robert greatly enjoyed getting to know his younger sister better.

> *My mother-in-law was with me during all four of my births and when she was sitting next to me holding my hand during the cesareans, well, I craved that.*
>
> —Patricia Heaton

Questions for Discussion

❀ Do you have any siblings whose lives seem very different from your own?

_____

_____

❀ If you both have children now, do you think it will make it easier for you to relate to each other?

_____

_____

❀ If you come from a large family, are you more in contact with siblings with whom you didn't interact very often before?

_____

❀ With which person in your family do you most hope that the birth of your new baby will help you forge a new or better relationship? What are you hoping for, and how long do you think it will take to improve your relationship?

> ### Take Action!
> Strengthen family connections with siblings, cousins, and grandparents by seeking their advice about raising children. Let them know how important their wisdom and experience are to you. You'll be glad you sought out this connection with your extended family, especially if you have not had a close relationship in the past due to differing interests.

When you look at your life, the greatest happinesses are family happinesses.

—Dr. Joyce Brothers

CONCLUSION

Do you remember good times with siblings and cousins when you were a child? Often, our fondest childhood memories consist of those times spent with our relatives at family get-togethers. Don't let your child miss out on the same experiences! Take the time to get reacquainted with extended family members and build bonds between you. You'll be glad you did, and you'll be giving your child a lifetime of wonderful memories!

Six

A Baby . . . Will Cause
You to Examine Your Beliefs—
and Question Your Faith

> However we understand or speak of this mystery, that first year of your baby's life will teach you that there is no "randomness" or "chance" to the pairing of you with your child.

Who cannot be moved by the sight of a precious little baby? When you first see that tiny being enter the world, you know that you'll never see anything more wondrous and amazing. Even your heart is in for a surprise as it falls in love in a way it has never experienced! Perhaps you even noticed that, upon sighting this new little life, the doctor present at the birth of your baby recognized a miracle in action—and this doctor delivers babies day in and day out! Yes, a baby will help you discover a wellspring of love within you that you never thought possible. This little being is yours, a work of art crafted just for you—a one-of-a-kind. There has never been and will never be another baby just like yours. Even if you have identical twins, you will know they are not exactly the same when their personalities begin to emerge.

And to think that you were chosen to be the mother or father of this particular baby. It's an awe-inspiring concept, to be sure. However we understand or speak of this mystery, that first year of your baby's life will teach you that there is no randomness or chance to the pairing of you with your child. Only through the wisdom of something greater than our own understanding has this perfect match been made. If you don't believe it, just consult your heart! There is that feeling of amazement at the mere sight of the child—the miracle of it all. "Thank you," our hearts cry out. "Thank you for the life of this child, and for the feelings of overwhelming love inside my heart." And we use this faith even more as our thoughts turn to protecting this fragile little being and keeping her safe—an all-consuming job in the first year of life. How many parents find themselves alongside the crib of their feverish baby in the middle of the night, pleading, "Please, God, make her better," or simply basking in the beauty and glory of their child, only to hear themselves utter the words, "Thank you, God"?

Parents will further call upon faith as they cope with the trying times of baby's first year, and later when they search for guidance and answers as they lead their child through the trials of life. More and more, they find themselves recognizing the need for a spiritual and moral foundation for their child. They may begin looking for a house of worship in search of community and family. Those who don't believe in God may feel that the miraculous gift they've been given is proof of a Creator. Those who have wandered from their faith may be led to renew their trust and faith. Having a baby is a time of new beginnings in many ways. Of course, there will be times when difficulties arise. At such times, parents' faith may be tested. They may experience a crisis of faith—or they may find themselves leaning on God even more.

> *A baby is "a sweet new blossom of humanity, fresh fallen from God's own home, to flower on Earth."*
>
> —Gerald Massey

David and Erica had been married three years before they decided to have a child. Erica was raised in the Episcopalian Church, but David didn't practice any particular religion. Because Erica hadn't been attending church services, they didn't see religion as an issue that affected their relationship, or their lives for that matter. Nevertheless, they did briefly discuss how they would handle it once they had children. "When we have kids," Erica asked David, "what will we teach them about faith?" David assured Erica that they'd deal with it when the time came. Erica understood that to mean that it didn't really matter to David, and therefore if she later decided to have their baby dedicated in her Christian faith or attend a church, he wouldn't be opposed.

Six months before she got pregnant, Erica got a job at a Christian publishing company. The company motto was, "We practice what we print." Employees were encouraged to discuss issues of faith and share their beliefs with each other. Erica became more and more intrigued. As she became more involved in the faith-based spirit of her job, she decided to get reacquainted with her family's religious traditions. Although David didn't share in her enthusiasm, he nevertheless supported her interests as she began attending church and Bible studies.

Then baby Joshua was born. As Erica continued to grow in her faith, she desired to become more involved with her church and to raise Joshua as a Christian. But to her surprise, when she broached the subject to David, he was hesitant to agree. "I don't think we should impose any religious beliefs on our son," said David. "We should leave it up to him to decide when he's old enough." But this wasn't satisfying to Erica. "I want our baby to have God's blessings," she told him. "I feel really strongly about this. It's important to me, and I want to arrange for Joshua to be baptized." So the faith issue became important. It was hard enough for Erica not being able to share her joy in God with her husband, but not to experience it with her child was unimaginable to her.

FOUR WAYS A BABY WILL PUT
YOUR SPIRITUAL LIFE TO THE TEST

Although David and Erica's religious beliefs had never been an issue between them in the past, the arrival of a child suddenly shoved the question of their beliefs to the forefront. The religious differences that they had put on the back burner would become critical to their relationship as they raised a son together.

> *Faith is like radar that sees through the fog— the reality of things at a distance that the human eye cannot see.*
>
> —Corrie Ten Boom

131

Their child belonged to both of them—and yet their unity was jeopardized by the religious differences between them. Their experience is indicative of the types of spiritual issues that often confront couples who have a child.

A Baby Will Cause You to Question the Role of Faith in Your Life

It's not uncommon these days for people of different faiths or religious traditions to marry. Even if they were both raised in a particular faith, one or both of them may not be very active in his or her religious life, so it seldom creates problems for the couple—until they have children. Once it comes down to deciding which faith—if any—the child will be raised in and whether or not he or she will be dedicated or baptized, this issue becomes more real to the couple. We know a woman who was raised in the Roman Catholic faith and was very active in her church. She married a man who was Russian Orthodox, but since he seldom attended services, he had agreed before their marriage that any children could be raised in the Catholic Church. Therefore, the woman was shocked to discover that he had sneaked their infant children over to the Russian Orthodox church to be baptized shortly after their births! Obviously, even though this couple thought that things had been worked out to their mutual satisfaction prior to having children, there was still a conflict.

Erica, too, was shocked that David had misgivings about having Joshua baptized. "The church stresses the importance of dedicating children," Erica told him. "Why wouldn't you want our son baptized?" When he put off discussing religion before they married, she had assumed it was just because he was indifferent about the issue. In truth, he was just putting off the inevitable decision and was hoping that things would somehow be resolved by the time children came along. But with the birth of their baby, this unresolved issue became a big problem for the couple.

Questions for Discussion

● Have you and your partner discussed what religion—if any— you will raise your child in?

132

_____

_____

❀ If you practice the same religion, have you discussed how active you plan to be as a family in your place of worship?

_____

_____

❀ Have your families pressured you to follow a particular religious path?

_____

_____

❀ How will you resolve any differences that you and your partner have in terms of religion?

_____

_____

> ### Take Action!
>
> If you and your partner are having difficulties resolving issues of faith, parental counseling may be in order. Because religion is often a hot-button issue for many people, involving very strong emotions, the neutrality of a counselor's office is often necessary for looking at things objectively and coming to an agreement.

Erica and David decided to visit a family counselor to help them resolve their differences. During their sessions, David discussed with Erica the particular objections he had about belonging to a church. "It's not that I don't believe in God," he told Erica. "I just don't like the whole structured approach to practicing religion. Why can't I just look for God in a beautiful sunset, or better yet, in the face of my child?" To David's surprise, Erica ex-

My husband and I divorced over religious differences. He thought he was God, and I didn't.

—seen on a t-shirt

133

pressed understanding of his position—and encouraged him to continue seeking God outside of church—but she also told David that not all churches were created equal. Perhaps the churches that David had experienced in his life had felt repressive to him, but another one may not. They discussed the advantages of providing Joshua with more spiritual grounding than David had. Although David was still skeptical at first, he agreed to be open-minded and began attending services with Erica. He couldn't say that he loved it the first few times he attended, but as he got to know more people and considered himself a part of the church family, he started to see why Erica was drawn to the church. He couldn't deny that she certainly seemed more relaxed and joyful after going to the services! Perhaps this was something they could share as a family after all.

Faith May Get Put on the Back Burner

For many parents, faith can get put on the back burner when a child arrives. You're so busy dealing with this beautiful—but very demanding—being that you don't really have time for God. If things are going well, you may even take things for granted, thinking you don't need God "right now." And if you're having trouble coping, most likely you'll consult with your doctor, parents, friends, or siblings, never even thinking that help is just a prayer away! But think about it: Have you ever thought of asking God for help with the challenges of parenting? When you're having a bad day—or night—do you ask God to give you strength to get through that trying time? Do you make use of the comfort and leadership that faith can provide?

> *When the solution is simple, God is answering.*
>
> —Albert Einstein

Because he didn't consider himself faith-based, David never considered turning his problems over to God. He relied upon himself to deal with the problems of life. As someone who had lived most of his life without religion, he had become accustomed to being self-reliant and keeping things to himself—all the while feeling more and more alone in the process. As happy as David was when Joshua arrived, it didn't occur to him to see God as the grantor of this blessing and therefore to be grateful to Him. Nor did it occur to him to seek guidance when the daily grind of parenting hit. It just wasn't his way.

Questions for Discussion

❀ Do you believe that faith can help people get through difficult times or the day-to-day stresses of life?

_____

_____

❀ Have you ever sought guidance from a Higher Power during stressful periods? How did it make you feel?

_____

_____

❀ Who do you consult first with a parenting problem? Have you considered that God can help?

_____

_____

> ### Take Action!
> Whenever you're grappling with issues of faith, you need to seek answers and support. Call a house of worship and ask to speak with a spiritual leader or counselor. Search for answers in the Bible or other spiritual readings. Talk to people who are strong in faith. Most of all, pray for peace and understanding.

As David began to explore his faith once again, he felt less alone. He would find himself talking to God in his head when he was having a bad day at work or fighting traffic on the way home. And when he and Erica were concerned about Joshua or lacked confidence in a parenting decision, they sought guidance from God. Somehow it was very comforting for David, although he felt uncomfortable at first. But he noticed that, for the first time in his life, he felt more at peace and less at war with the world.

You May Expect Too Much from God

Although David was just beginning to learn to turn to God, there are others who use God as a magic genie, expecting Him to meet all of their needs and answer all of their pleas. Instead of making the effort to tackle life's challenges through their own initiative, they forget that God equipped them with the skills to make their own choices. Rather than doing the necessary research to solve their problems, they continually ask God to give them a sign and make the decision for them. But as the old saying goes, "God helps those who help themselves." When we rely too much on God, we fail to grow ourselves. We don't become the grown-ups whom God designed us to be.

Erica realized that she had to be proactive in handling the situation with David. She was so busy looking for a lightning bolt to hit David in the head with sudden understanding—fervently pleading with God to make things right and get David to see the light—that she failed at first to see that David didn't necessarily understand the celebrations of her faith. "What's so important about baptism?" he'd asked, time and time again. Realizing that he really didn't know the answer, she explained, "In my faith, dedicating a baby is a ceremony, a commitment for parents to raise their child with Christian values and a Christian lifestyle." Erica also realized that God was already at work in David's life. Through counseling and their church experiences, God was slowly working on David's heart to bring about lasting changes.

Questions for Discussion

❀ Have you ever called upon God for help and become discouraged when it seemed as though He hadn't solved your problems?

_____

_____

❀ In what ways can we rely too much on God? Why can this be a bad thing to do?

_____

_____

❀ In what ways does God answer our prayers? Do we often miss the signs?

_____

_____

❀ In what ways are you asking God to be your genie?

_____

_____

Take Action!

Learn to recognize the presence of God in your life. See Him in the small nudges you hear in your brain or the coincidental phone call from an old friend. Realize that God is counting on you to heed His call and follow through. Don't expect God to solve all your problems. God wants us to learn self-reliance. The next time you have a problem, ask God not what He plans to do, but what He wants you to do.

Erica really felt that God was moving in their lives. No, He didn't strike David in the head and make him a sudden believer. But He led her to the right counselor and allowed David to feel God's presence as they attended church together. She asked God for patience and wisdom in bringing her family closer to Him, and she was shown the way.

You May Feel As If You "Don't Have Time" for God

Especially in that first year of a child's life, it's hard to imagine fitting one more thing into your schedule. Even the worthy pursuits—such as joining a Bible study or organizing or helping out at a fundraiser for charity—seem like just too much on your plate when you're caring for a baby. And church services aren't always scheduled at a time that works with the baby's naps and feedings. Who wants to wake up a sleeping baby to go to

> _Faith is not day-dreaming; it is decision-making!_
>
> —Robert Schuller

church when he'll just fuss once you're there? It's common to put religious activities on hold because they're just not convenient when you have a child.

When Joshua was young, Erica was overwhelmed with his care and rarely found the time to go to church. Because David didn't initially share her faith, it also made attending church a lonely experience. Despite David's disapproval, she wanted to take Joshua with her, but then she found it difficult to deal with his fussy behavior all by herself. It just seemed like more hassle than it was worth. And if she couldn't make it to church, she certainly couldn't envision attending any other church activities! Because of David's lack of support and the many demands on her time because Joshua was so young, feeding her faith fell to the bottom of her to-do list for a while.

Questions for Discussion

❀ Have your religious activities been put aside or decreased because of your more complicated schedule?

_____

_____

❀ How can you find the time to devote to God in your busy life? Have you thought about different ways of continuing your relationship with God?

_____

_____

❀ Do you think that you'll be able to resume more religious activities when your child is older? What is your plan for doing so?

_____

_____

> ### Take Action!
> Your house of worship may have all kinds of opportunities for service that don't necessarily require huge blocks of your time. If it has a nursery, perhaps you can volunteer there once a month and bring your child with you. (And take advantage of this same nursery when you attend services.) Volunteer to be part of a prayer committee in which you pray for the needs of people in your religious community. Maybe your church needs help with something you can do at home, like putting together mailings or making phone calls. Never assume that you don't have time until you find out what opportunities are available. You may be pleasantly surprised to find that you can still be involved.

Realistically, Erica certainly did have less time in Joshua's early months, but she soon found out there were other ways to continue to grow in her faith. For instance, Erica set aside ten minutes for devotional reading each evening at bedtime. She also learned about a mothers' group at her church to which mothers brought their young children and discussed issues of faith. They told her about a program in which she could put together care packages at home to give to the homeless. As Erica was able to become more involved in church activities, she actually felt she was making better use of her precious time.

With two small boys, I've never found it so difficult to spend time with the Lord. Normally the boys are running all over the place, and there are toys everywhere. It's mayhem around here. So I totally get it when women say to me, "How am I supposed to spend time with God? I have four kids." Girl, I don't even know!

—Priscilla Shirer, author of And We Are Changed and A Jewel in His Crown

FIVE WAYS A BABY WILL ENHANCE
YOUR SPIRITUAL LIFE

For many parents, the experience of having a child brings them closer to God. In the least, it makes them a believer in miracles. And they know that a miracle was granted and they're in awe. Sheer awe. If you don't believe it, just ask any parent who has just watched the birth of his child! And this miracle has happened, has been granted, to you!

What greater gift can there be than to become a parent? Whatever religion you may practice—or even if you practice no religion at all—you recognize the miracle of birth. First, there was just the two of you, and then suddenly there were three! And you and your partner actually created this being—with a little help from God. Wow! It's the rare person who is not moved by this incredible phenomenon.

You'll Feel the Need to Say "Thank You
for This Amazing Gift!"

Yes, a child is truly a miracle—a gift in our lives. We often feel a resurgence of love for the Creator when we have a child of our own. How blessed we are to have this precious experience! Especially if you've struggled with infertility, you can't deny the incredible blessing you've been given. You want to praise the heavens for granting it to you.

Despite his lack of faith in the past, David couldn't help feeling his heart fill with love when he saw that Joshua's eyes lit up when his daddy walked in the room. He couldn't deny that he'd been given an enormous gift and was privileged to be little Joshua's father. He began to see how truly blessed he was—a sign he took to mean that it was time to explore the source of his blessings. When Joshua's first word was "Da-da," David's heart overflowed with love. How could he fail to show gratitude for such a precious child? He began to feel as though he wanted God to, as his wife had said, bless his child. He wanted to be a good father in time and do all he could to raise this little boy in the best way possible. And though at first he didn't know how or who could help him do that, it wasn't long before he was turning his prayers heavenward. Perhaps, he felt, God had a plan for his child—and maybe even for himself. He was positive that he wanted God to look out for his child, and he was no longer hesitant in asking God to do that. In time, all these new and wonderful feelings of knowing that he was meant to be the father of this child helped him find his way to expressing his appreciation to the Force in the Universe that made it all happen for him.

Questions for Discussion

❀ Do you see your child as a blessing—a gift—from God?

_____

_____

❀ Do you see the creation of a child as a miracle?

_____

_____

❀ Do you feel a greater spiritual connection through the process of having a child?

_____

_____

❀ Have you thanked God for allowing you to become a parent?

_____

_____

Take Action!

Do something to honor the miracle of life you've been given. For example, plant a little tree in your yard and watch it grow taller and stronger each year, just as your child does! Mark your child's height each year on the bark of the tree. Make it an annual tradition on your child's birthday to go out to "Isaac's tree" or "Jessica's tree."

You'll Feel the Need to Provide Your
Child with a Moral, Spiritual Upbringing

Oftentimes, having a child can bring about a resurgence of your religious faith. Most parents recognize that they can use all the help they can get to give their children a good moral grounding in today's world. Often, joining a house of worship is seen as a step in the right direction. If you were lax about attending services in the past, you feel that now's the time to walk the talk and practice what you preach. One mother told us that she felt an "instant identification of my daughter as a soul; therefore she belonged to God, and God was calling on me to be a spiritual mentor to this child."

Erica not only wanted a religious experience for her child, but she recognized that her church could provide the support that she needed to raise Joshua to be a secure and loving person. Even David had to admit that Erica seemed more at peace since her return to faith—and he wanted that same experience for the whole family. When he was growing up, David saw an older brother turn to drugs and alcohol to get through the pains of life. David had often wondered if things might have turned out differently for his brother if their family had been more spiritually grounded. When his brother joined Alcoholics Anonymous—when he began to "let go and let God"—he was able to work through a recovery program and stay clean and sober. Recalling this experience led David to believe that raising Joshua in the church was better than giving him no religious background at all. In time, it was David who encouraged his wife to contact the church for the dedication of his son—now feeling that having their son baptized was the right thing to do.

Questions for Discussion

❀ Why do some people resume their religious practices when they become parents?

_____

_____

❀ What are the benefits to a family of belonging to a religious institution?

_____

● How does a belief in God help parents in raising their children?

● Can having faith help you get through difficult times in life?

● What spiritual values do you hope to impart to your children?

> ### Take Action!
> If you wish to find a house of worship where you'll feel at home, begin your search. Take recommendations from friends about the places they attend. Choose a different place to attend each week. Look especially for congregations that have lots of family activities and groups for children. Make sure the membership is growing. Do you enjoy the sermons? Are the people happy and friendly? Do they hang around after the service or rush out to the parking lot without a word to each other? Once you decide to join a church family, get involved! Call and ask how you can contribute. It's the best way to get to know people and become an active member.

You'll Pray More

If, in the past, your prayers consisted of memorized "Our Fathers" and quickly worded pleas, you may find your prayers expanding when you have a child. There's so much more to say to God: "Thank you for this beautiful child!" "Please keep my

> *Church isn't where you meet. Church isn't a building. Church is what you do. Church is who you are.*
>
> —Bridget Willard

> *He prayeth best who loveth best.*
>
> —Samuel Taylor Coleridge

son healthy and safe." "Please bring peace to all countries so that my child can grow up in a loving world." "Show me how to raise a happy and healthy daughter." You have so much to be thankful for, but also so many more worries and concerns. Life feels safer when you ask God to accompany you along the way. And not only do you feel the need to protect your child, but because you feel that God holds you responsible for your child's upbringing, you are even more diligent about protecting yourself!

Erica said, "I drive more carefully now—even when I don't have Joshua with me. I have to keep my baby alive, yes, but it's my responsibility to keep his mother—me!—alive too, so that I can be there for my baby." Erica also felt the form of her prayers changing. She found that her prayers were more for Joshua and less for herself. If her child was well and happy, she no longer needed anything for herself. And she asked for God's blessing of Grandma and Grandpa and for the well-being of other family members on both sides of the family. She wanted her son to share in the love and comfort of family—and she knew that much of this was also up to God.

Questions for Discussion

● Have you started praying more now that you are a parent?

_____

_____

● Has the content of your prayers changed? In what ways? Do you ask for guidance and wisdom in parenting?

_____

_____

● Do you offer thanksgiving more, feeling gratitude and joy for your child?

_____

_____

● Do you pray together with your partner? If not, have you considered it?

_____

❁ How can you increase the time you spend in prayer?

> ### Take Action!
>
> Start a prayer journal. List the people and the things you wish to pray for. Most importantly, note those times when you receive an answer from God. When you prayed to find the best daycare facility for your child, were you led to the right place? Did someone who was ill pull through their crisis? If you were torn between career paths, did you feel a pull in a particular direction? By doing this exercise, you'll be amazed to see how actively God is involved in your life. He may not always give you your heart's desire, but He will lead you down the path that is right for you—if you are listening.

You'll Feel as Though the Raising of Your Child Is Being Shared by God

One young mother told us, "If nothing I did could soothe my baby or take away her teething pains, if my patience with her fussiness was becoming thin, I'd find myself calling God to my side, saying, 'Okay, God, what do I do here?' or even 'Think you could take over for a while here, God?' And, always, I felt peace. Knowing God was right there was calming, and I felt centered." Like this mother, parents may see raising children as a job shared with God—something they go through together, never alone. God gives them the ability to handle what comes, to get them through the trying times of parenting, to have confidence in their decisions. And to turn over what they cannot change or fix on their own.

Erica felt God's loving hand on her shoulder as she coped with the difficulties of parenting Joshua. She began to understand the great love that God had for her when she experienced such unconditional love for her own child. She would do anything to keep Joshua safe, to protect him, and to ensure that he had every opportunity in life. She knew that God was looking out for her and David in the same way. She experienced a peace that she had never felt before.

Questions for Discussion

❀ Do you experience God as a loving father—a "co-parent"?

_____

_____

❀ Do you understand God's love for you better now that you are a parent?

_____

_____

❀ Does it comfort you to know that you have a "third parent" on your parenting team?

_____

_____

Take Action!

Think about your own parents. Do you understand them and their choices better now that you're a parent? Let them know that you appreciate all the sacrifices they made for you. If you feel uncomfortable talking to them, then say it in a card or letter. Don't let the opportunity pass to tell your parents how much they mean to you.

You'll Believe in Innocence Again

Considering all the difficulties and troubles in the world, it's easy to become cynical and hardened. It's tough to look on the bright side when every headline screams about another injustice or tragedy. But somehow, having a child can help us perceive the world in a new way. It can give us hope for the future of the world. One mother told us, "Before I had the baby, I was beginning to feel a bit jaded about life, and that tainted all of my interactions with people. My to-do list was ever-present and that seemed to direct my energy. The price I paid was that I was often short with people, even aloof and mostly uninterested in other people's lives, and often forgot the real joy of being alive! But my baby was so innocent and pure. I loved the way her eyes shone and just danced when she saw me. Her entire little body seemed to experience the joy of just seeing her mommy walk in the room. I wondered what little things still brought such delight to my heart. And did my eyes still sparkle? Just standing still and watching my baby made me feel as if God had sent her my way to help restore my belief in innocence and the importance of joy and simple abundance. It made me think, 'Oh, I've got to regain a bit of this purity in my life!' It was a balm to my heart and soul that I couldn't have found anywhere else."

> *How great is the love the Father has lavished on us, that we should be called children of God!*
> —1 John 3:1

David, too, had been feeling a bit beaten down by life. Everywhere he turned, it seemed as if someone wanted something from him—and he couldn't possibly please them all. He had lost so much faith in mankind, but he had yet to discover faith in God. It was a harsh and mostly selfish world that he had to tackle alone. But when Joshua was born, it was as if he had been given a new start and a reason to meet the daily grind and surmount the ordinary—and to find great purpose in it. And the joy was returning. As the baby grew and became more aware of his surroundings, David began to see the little delights in his world. Hearing Joshua say a word for the first time or smack his lips from the taste of his baby food or delight in seeing funny faces showed David that there was still joy and goodness in the world—

> *I am ready to meet my Maker. Whether my Maker is prepared for the ordeal of meeting me is another matter.*
>
> —Winston Churchill

right under his nose, in fact. Joshua's zest for life reignited David's own enthusiasm for the world in which he lived, and he learned to take off the dark glasses through which he'd been viewing things and feel the need to be enthusiastic about showing his son that the world was safe and fun. And he knew he wanted to share and teach and fill his son with love and the wonder of being alive.

Questions for Discussion

❁ In what ways does the innocence of a child introduce us to the delights of the world?

_____

_____

❁ Do you think you're more optimistic about life now that you have a child?

_____

_____

❁ How does the birth of a child help our own souls to be reborn?

_____

_____

❁ Do you remember to capture the joy in special moments?

_____

_____

> **Take Action!**
> Everything in the world is fresh and new to your child. The feel of sand between her toes, the raindrops falling on the roof, the smell of flowers in the garden—all are new discoveries for her! Make a vow to yourself to re-discover something new each day. If it's raining, turn off the TV (especially the news!) and listen to the rain-drops on the roof. Take a detour on the way home from work through neighborhoods you've never visited be-fore. Shut off talk radio and listen to a CD of beautiful hymns—or put in your baby's CD and learn the silly sounds! Bake a batch of cookies and delight in their aroma. Enjoy them with a mug of hot chocolate and marshmallows. Learn to find joy in life again.

CONCLUSION

We take spiritual steps every day of our lives: sometimes backward, other times forward. You may find yourself taking a lot of steps in either direction when you have a child. Whether you experience a crisis—or a resurgence—of faith, it is a time to examine your beliefs and feelings with the goal of seeking resolution. It is also an opportunity for you and your partner not only to resolve your differences, but also to grow together in the direction of greater faith—in whatever form you agree on. When you establish family traditions and practices grounded in faith, you strengthen your bond as a family and come to understand the true of meaning of "Love one another."

Seven

Friends and Your Baby: You'll Make Many . . . and Lose a Few!

> Being parents opens up a whole new world of friendships.

Of course, your friends are happy for you when you have a baby. When they hear you're expecting, they want to throw a shower, make inquiries about your health, and engage in dialogue about the baby's name. But when the baby arrives, things can change. This isn't necessarily a negative event. Sometimes your friendships become even stronger if you share the parenting experience. You may delight in getting together with your children and form a stronger bond through this connection. On the other hand, you may begin to feel like you're trying to keep up with the Joneses as other parents start comparing notes on whose baby reached a particular milestone first. And your relationships with childless friends may also be put to the test. Some friends are thrilled to be "aunt" or "uncle" to your bundle of joy. But others may grow impatient with your preoccupation with your child and your sudden lack of availability or topics of conversation other than your baby. All of our lives, friendships come and go as our circumstances change. The arrival of a new baby just happens to be one of those critical times.

Marilee and Cathy had been best friends ever since they were roommates during their freshman year of college. Both were from the Midwest, majoring in education, and playing in the college band. Because they shared the same interests and took many of the same classes, it was just a matter of time before the girls described themselves as "practically sisters" and "two peas in a pod." After college, they moved to separate states, but continued to stay in contact. Marilee took a teaching job in south Florida, while Cathy went east to accept a position as an educational consultant for a large software firm. They stayed in contact by phone and e-mails, discussing everything from the men they were dating to the best ways to get ahead in their respective careers. Cathy would visit Marilee several times a year in Florida, and Marilee came to see Cathy in Pennsylvania whenever her teaching schedule gave her a break. Even though they were miles and miles apart, their relationship felt as fresh as if they were still roommates.

When Marilee became engaged to Brock, she chose Cathy as her maid of honor. Cathy was happy to accept. She was thrilled that Marilee had found a wonderful man and couldn't be happier for her. Two years later, Marilee became pregnant. Again, Cathy was excited for her friend, although she couldn't help feeling a little jealous that Marilee was going to be a mother—something that she too had dreamed about experiencing some day. Of course, when they talked on the phone, Marilee couldn't help but share her excitement with her closest friend—and, it seemed to Cathy, every minute detail about each development in her pregnancy.

It didn't occur to Marilee that this would be seen as anything other than sharing her spectacular joy with her best friend, but Cathy began to see things another way. "I started to not answer the phone when I saw Marilee's number because it seemed like she only wanted to talk about her pregnancy," Cathy said. Marilee would gush, "We got to hear the baby's heartbeat today!" or "Brock's so cute, making sure we buy the very safest car seat!" It was all getting to be a little bit much for Cathy. Marilee's visits stopped because she didn't feel comfortable traveling so far from home while pregnant, and Cathy really didn't feel like accepting Marilee's invitation to come down and help her decorate the baby's room. She was happy that her friend now had the life that she wanted, but it seemed to her that Marilee didn't have the same patience for what was going on in Cathy's life. Cathy said, "One day when Marilee called, I tried to talk to her about my troubled love life, but she just shrugged it off by saying, 'Oh, don't worry about it, Cathy. Your prince will come! Just relax!' It wasn't really the kind of empathetic advice I wanted to hear. I just felt our relationship had changed so much and that we no longer had much in common."

When baby Ben arrived, Cathy and Marilee grew even further apart. Every conversation with Marilee started out with, "You should see the cute thing the baby did today . . ." or "Gosh, I'm so exhausted from being up all night!" As the phone calls and e-mails became less frequent, Marilee started meeting up with some of the other young mothers in her neighborhood. Several of the teachers at the school where she taught were also mothers, so they would get together at the park with their kids or share babysitting services. Marilee finally convinced Cathy to come down to Florida for the baby's christening, but Cathy had a miserable time hanging out with Marilee's new friends. She couldn't help feeling like a fifth wheel and, as it turned out, flew back home two days sooner than originally planned.

That first year of Ben's life had a dramatic impact on Cathy and Marilee's friendship. The girls now had so little in common. Marilee was shopping for baby clothes and supplies; Cathy was shopping for a trip to Paris with her friends. Marilee was heating bottles and making quick meals to eat; Cathy was eating at restaurants with exciting clients via the privilege of an expense account. Marilee spent her weekends at home in babyproof clothes like sweat suits and t-shirts; Cathy had a nice wardrobe that got a lot of use on the weekends. Cathy was still "Cathy," but Marilee had morphed into "Ben's Mom." Even after Ben celebrated his first birthday and life calmed down a bit for Marilee and Brock, their child would always be the primary focus of their lives and activities. But although Cathy had difficulty taking a back seat to Marilee's new family, in time she and Marilee found new ways to connect with each other.

> *My children are my first priority.*
>
> —Denise Richards

153

FIVE WAYS A BABY WILL CHALLENGE
YOUR FRIENDSHIPS

Our lives are always evolving, and it's a rare person who finds herself with the same priorities all her life. At one point in your life, your schooling is your top priority. At another, perhaps it's your career or travel. At still another, it's dating and finding a life partner. Most of us come to a time in our lives when being a parent becomes our Number One focus. This is natural and inevitable. Cathy will most likely have a child someday, whether she becomes pregnant or adopts, but she and Marilee will forevermore be at different stages in life. Having less in common and changing priorities have had a critical effect on their friendship.

You'll No Longer Be in Sync: Your Preoccupation with Your Child Will Not Be Shared by Friends

It's not at all uncommon for new parents to discover that their child dominates their daily lives. Children are, after all, in need of 24/7 protection, care, and love. Just as a married couple may find they've grown apart when their days become overtaken by the constant responsibility of caring for a child, a friendship can also suffer from growing pains. When your friends don't have children, or if their children are much older than yours, you may find that your interests are no longer in sync, which is what happened with Marilee and Cathy.

When Marilee became pregnant, and then joined the ranks of motherhood, her focus naturally shifted to her child. Of course, Cathy couldn't relate. Her priority was her career and social life. She felt like a fish out of water around Marilee and had little to contribute to the conversation when Marilee started talking about baby bottles, playgroups, and babysitters. Though she didn't admit it to Marilee, these things simply did not interest her. She wasn't married, and children were the furthest thing from her mind—even if hearing the joy in Marilee's voice sometimes made her wonder what she was missing. Marilee, on the other hand, cared about her friend's career advancement, but felt she had moved on from that stage in her life and didn't understand why Cathy was still so hung up on the need to live such a hectic lifestyle. Because the two friends were no longer living their lives in the same way, they had little to talk about anymore.

Marilee's husband Brock was also experiencing this problem with his friends. In the coffee room at work, his buddies would be talking about the movies they had seen the previous weekend or planning "Tournament Day" to play eighteen holes of golf. With his wife needing time away from the around-the-clock demands of their ten-month-old baby, an all-day event at the golf course was a thing of the past for Brock—at least for now. And when the sales team met to divvy up the accounts, Brock knew he'd mostly be working with other new fathers because they, like him, were no longer interested in spending a lot of time on the road. Although Brock had enjoyed common interests with many of the men on the sales team before, he noticed that their allegiance to him was changing. Whereas most of them got together now and then for a drink after work, he rarely took part in these gatherings anymore because he had to (and wanted to!) get home to Ben. Although this was his choice, he still couldn't help feeling a little left out of the conversation when he couldn't debate the merits of the latest Spider-Man movie or put in his two cents on which bar served the best martinis.

Questions for Discussion

❋ Did your relationship with friends who are not parents change when you got pregnant or had a baby? What about your relationship with friends who were already parents?

_____

_____

❋ Think about your best friend. What things do you have in common? Do you and your friend still share the same interests now that you're a mother?

_____

_____

❋ In what ways will your priorities shift after having a baby in terms of friendship? Do you think your friends will still be as high on your priority list?

_____

> ## Take Action!
> If staying in touch with your friends is important to you (and we hope it is!), make a point to continue to develop your interests outside of motherhood. If you and a friend always shared a love of cooking, let your friend know you still value your friendship by signing up for a cooking class together at a time when your husband is available to watch the baby. Let your friend know that even though your baby is now your Number One priority, you're still very interested in maintaining your relationship her.

Although Marilee and Cathy accepted that their friendship would never be the same as they continued to move in different directions, they did not want to lose their shared connection to the past. When they received news that their sorority was hosting a reunion, they met in their old college town and shared a hotel room just like in the old days. At this point, Ben had celebrated his first birthday, and Marilee felt more comfortable leaving him for a longer period of time. She and Cathy made a pact to leave home behind and just enjoy themselves as young friends again. They visited many of the old restaurants and other places where they used to hang out in college and had a great trip down memory lane. It was good for Marilee to put aside her mothering responsibilities for a few days, and Cathy enjoyed just having her best girlfriend to hang out with again!

As for Brock, he made an effort to get to know some of the people at work who were also parents—guys he had spent little time with before because they were rarely available for social engagements. When visiting someone's desk, he'd make it a point to engage in small talk when he saw pictures of their children. When he and Marilee started pricing family vehicles, he consulted his coworkers who had minivans parked in the company parking lot.

You'll Be Too Busy to Hang Out with Your Friends

Most people comment after their baby's first six months of life, "I've never been so exhausted in my life!" Leisure time goes out the window when you're feeding, changing, consoling, loving, and ferrying a little child. And during those rare times when the baby decides to sleep, you're too tired to do anything other than catch a few winks yourself or veg out in front of the television. Your new busy schedule leaves very little time for cultivating and nurturing friendships, as Marilee and Cathy found.

Marilee's trips to Pennsylvania to visit Cathy were no longer possible when she became pregnant and had the baby. She had too much to do trying to juggle a job and motherhood. She just didn't see how she could fit an out-of-town trip into her schedule when she barely had time to clean the house and get the groceries. Besides, Marilee really had no interest in being away from her baby in that first year. As a working mother, she didn't want to miss a moment of her baby's development. If she were out of town when her baby uttered his first word, she would never forgive herself! And she knew that bringing Ben along was not an option. She and Cathy would never be able to relax and do activities together if they had to work around a baby's schedule. Besides, she had the sense that Ben wouldn't be entirely welcome at Cathy's place. Cathy tried to encourage Marilee to "take time for yourself," but Marilee wasn't ready to do that—not for more than a few hours at a time.

Brock also found himself too busy to hang out with friends as often as he once did. At the end of the day, he just wanted to go home and chill out! Some things had to be cut from his schedule, and when it came down to the choice of spending more time with Ben or going

> _You race home from the office to ferry your kids to soccer practice and piano, sling dinner on their plates, and wedge in a hurried chat with your husband before you nod off in front of your favorite TV show. Who has time for friends?_
>
> —Marla Paul in The Friendship Crisis: Finding, Making, and Keeping Friends When You're Not a Kid Anymore

Parenting magazine asked its readers, "When did you last have lunch, dinner, or even coffee with a friend—and without the kids?" It cited as good news the fact that 30 percent of its readers said "this week," but the bad news was that 38 percent couldn't remember!

out (something he'd done plenty of times in the past), he chose to stay home. He didn't want to miss any of Ben's growing-up years. Besides, he knew that Marilee had been alone with Ben for several hours after school, and he felt it was important to relieve her so she could have some time for herself. Like Marilee, Brock's time was no longer his own. For instance, he no longer had the option of spending Saturday in an all-day golf game with the boys. While he could make plans to get away now and then, the all-day Saturday every weekend was a thing of the past, at least for now. And his friends understood: They simply stopped asking if he was free to join them for these outings.

Questions for Discussion

● Do you find yourself losing contact with your friends because you're just too busy to do the things you used to do?

_____

_____

● Do you resent knowing that your friends can go to a last-minute movie or dinner, but you can't without finding a babysitter? Or have you "been there, done that," and are you content with a slower social life?

_____

_____

● Are your friends upset with you because they feel they're not as important to you anymore?

_____

_____

> ### Take Action!
>
> It's absolutely true that you'll have less time for other relationships when you have a baby. Taking care of a little one is a 24/7 job, even with your partner's help. So you need to be a little creative in preserving your friendships. Although you may not see each other as much, e-mail and the telephone can still help you keep in touch. Or you can ask a nearby friend to come over during naptime for a cup of coffee and a chat. Meet at the mall or a park and talk while you push the stroller. Most of all, be sensitive to the way your friends are feeling. Let them know that you still value their friendship even if you just drop a short note in the mail or leave a phone message. Your friends will surely treasure these little tokens of friendship.

Thank goodness for e-mail! Marilee managed to squeeze in e-mails to Cathy when the baby was sleeping. Sometimes she could send notes when she had a free moment at work. And Cathy accepted that during this phase of their friendship, they were most comfortable as e-mail friends. They still shared their wonderful memories, and that was enough for now to fill lots of messages! As Ben got older and more independent, Marilee found she had more free time to keep up her correspondence with Cathy.

Some Will Be Jealous That You're a Parent

For the friend who has suffered through infertility, miscarriages, or a disappointing love life, your beautiful, bouncing baby may just serve as a reminder that she doesn't have the joy of a baby—and you do. It's hard for her to sympathize when you're com-

My mom used to say it doesn't matter how many kids you have . . . because one kid'll take up 100 percent of your time so more kids can't possibly take up more than 100 percent of your time.

—Karen Brown

159

> *When I struggled with infertility for two years, it was just too painful for me to be around my friends who were new mommies. On the outside, I was smiling, but when I went home I'd burst into tears over the baby I thought I'd never have. I had to avoid these friends to maintain my sanity. When I finally had my son, I was able to rekindle these friendships.*
>
> —Abby Brooks, a new mother

plaining about getting up three times in one night when she would gladly do the same if only she could become a mother. It's not your fault that things haven't gone well for your friend—and certainly you're entitled to your own happiness even if your friend is not at the same stage of life—but recognize that the unfortunate side effect of your blessing may be the loss of time spent with a friend who just can't cope at the moment. And others may be envious of the way you've managed to recast your life. Suppose you have a healthy baby, maintain a happy marriage, and still find time for a satisfying career—in short, you seem to have it all; you may be the object of envy to those who struggle with all of the roles in their lives. A dad who splits from work and says, "Oh, man, I've so fallen in love with that girl of mine . . . she's cutting teeth and so cute it's unbelievable," is envied by the parent who isn't necessarily basking in the same role. And, of course, there are the glares from those women who are thinking, "I'm fat now that I've had the baby—and here you are back to wearing a size four after only three months." Any time one achieves a certain measure of success—through becoming a parent, finding a soulmate, or getting a promotion—there will be others in the wings thinking, "Why is it always so easy for her?" or "Why does she get all the breaks?"

Even though it was Cathy's choice to focus on her career for the time being, whenever she heard the joy in Marilee's voice about being a mother, she was reminded of what she just might be missing in her life. Cathy hoped to be a mom one day herself, but Marilee was enjoying motherhood now, while Cathy hadn't even met Mr. Right yet. Cathy didn't want to be jealous of Marilee's life, but she was.

Questions for Discussion

❀ Do any of your friends appear to be avoiding your company or making excuses not to stay in touch?

_____

_____

❀ Have you found that some friends aren't as supportive of your happiness as you'd thought they'd be?

_____

_____

❀ Is it possible that you may be dominating your conversations with talk about your child and alienating your friends who are childless or going through a difficult period in life?

_____

_____

❀ How can you help your jealous friends feel more comfortable around you and less resentful of your happiness?

_____

_____

Take Action!

Friends who are not yet mothers (and want to be), or who are struggling with infertility, will naturally be envious of your good fortune. Be sensitive to their feelings and avoid talking too much about your child. Although your natural inclination is to talk about the biggest love of your life, try to put yourself in your friends' shoes and imagine your feelings if the situation were reversed. Look for other topics of conversation and make a real effort to meet with your friends alone, even if it's only for a short period of time.

Cathy wrote a letter to Marilee and shared how sad she felt when Marilee talked a lot about being a mother. She apologized for her jealous feelings, but let Marilee know that she was just having a hard time dealing with it all. Marilee was surprised. Because she knew what a wonderful person Cathy was, she had never doubted that Cathy would one day get married and have children. She didn't realize that sharing her joy as well as complaining about her workload had seemed insensitive to Cathy. After receiving the letter, Marilee made an effort to focus more on other topics when she spoke with Cathy. They made a pact: Marilee could talk for two minutes about Ben and Cathy could talk for two minutes about her career—just enough time to share but not dominate the conversation. Then they moved on to other topics. Marilee was content to save her mommy talk for her other friends who were mothers. She didn't want to lose her friendship with Cathy and resolved to be more sympathetic to her feelings.

You'll Feel Guilty That You Can't Always Be There for Your Friends

Nothing brings on a guilt trip faster than having demands placed on you from all sides and feeling as if you're not meeting all of them. The baby needs you around the clock; your husband needs your attention; your friends want your time; your boss naturally sees you in the role as an employee and not a parent; and you need a little time to yourself! Do you ever feel as if you're surrounded by a sea of hands that are grabbing you from every direction? And the natural byproduct of trying to cope with it all is guilt when you fail, especially when it means that you're letting down your friends. When your friend Sarah is expecting you to help her shop for a wedding gown and you have to cancel because the baby is sick, you feel terrible about disappointing her. With friendship come obligation and responsibility, so when you can't follow through on your commitments to friends because your child's needs (understandably!) come first, it nevertheless can make you feel guilty about no longer being a good friend—always there for your pals.

Marilee and Brock both felt guilty at times about letting down their friends. As we've discussed, Marilee was emotionally less available to Cathy when she became a mother. And she found herself often saying no to other friends when they called to invite her out or asked for a favor. When a friend called with marital problems and Marilee had to cut short their conversation because Ben was screaming at the top of his lungs, she felt terrible about not being there for her friend. Brock, too, experienced his share of guilt when he dropped out of a planned fishing trip with his buddies because Marilee had to be at the countywide science fair with her students that weekend, so he had to stay home with Ben. Even though Marilee and Brock knew they'd made the right choices for their son, they still felt bad that their friends weren't getting as much from them as they'd had in the past.

> _Guilt: the gift that keeps on giving._
>
> —Erma Bombeck

Questions for Discussion

❀ Do you feel that you're being pulled in too many different directions, trying to meet everyone's needs and demands?

_____

_____

❀ Do you feel less emotionally available to your friends now?

_____

_____

❀ Do you feel bad that you don't have as much time to spend with your friends?

_____

_____

❀ Why do you think we have a heightened sense of guilt when we become parents?

_____

_____

> ### Take Action!
> Being there for your friends is still possible, but it may take a little more creativity. If you have to hang up on a friend to tend to your child, ask her if you can call her back later when the baby's asleep. If you don't have time to talk with a needy friend, send a quick card or e-mail expressing your concern. Some disappointments just can't be avoided. If you have to cancel plans, it may not be possible to make things up, but a sincere apology goes a long way in maintaining friendships. Let your friend know how much you'll miss her company and that she's still important to you.

Marilee and Brock had to work together to make it more possible for them to meet up with friends. For example, with Marilee's encouragement, Brock rejoined his friends on Thursday nights for a basketball game at the YMCA—something he'd given up when Ben was first born. Sure, he didn't make it every Thursday if he was just too tired or Marilee wasn't feeling well, but he felt like he was continuing to cultivate his friendships by joining in their games.

You'll Have to Listen to (a Lot of) One-Upmanship: "My Kid Did That Sooner Than Your Kid!"

Parents seem to be programmed to think that their children are surely the most accomplished, adorable, and superior beings in the world. That's to ensure that we take the very best care of them and protect them with our lives. But the unfortunate side effect is that some parents aren't content to keep their pride to themselves. They have to make sure the world knows that other children will never compare favorably to theirs. This can often drive a wedge between friends. Unfortunately, Marilee ran into such a person on a regular basis.

Although Marilee enjoyed her new friends and found it helpful to compare notes on parenting techniques, it wasn't always a pleasant experience. One of her neighbor friends whom she often ran into at the park loved to engage in what Marilee termed "Mommy Wars." It seemed that every time Marilee mentioned something that her baby had accomplished, her friend felt the need to one up her with her own story. "My Dora started walking at eight months!" she would exclaim. "I can't believe your child still isn't walking! Have you talked to the doctor about it?" Or she would brag about being able to stay home with her child all day, making Marilee feel bad about her choice to return to her teaching job. "I could never let another person raise my children," the neighbor would pronounce.

> *The problem with children is that you have to put up with their parents.*
> —Charles DeLint

Questions for Discussion

❀ Do you know another mother who engages in Mommy Wars? Do you know any fathers who engage in this type of one-upmanship?

_____

_____

❀ How do you handle this type of person?

_____

_____

❀ Why do you think this person feels the need to be in competition with you?

_____

_____

❀ What can you say the next time this person tries to one-up you?

_____

_____

> ### Take Action!
> Yes, we all know parents who engage in competition with other parents, but examine your own behavior to make sure you're not contributing to discussions of this kind. It's always so tempting to brag about our children because they are, indeed, the most wonderful children in the world! But resist the temptation to proclaim this to everyone if you don't enjoy hearing others do the same. Teach yourself to experience joy in hearing about other children's accomplishments, just as you would want others to be happy about your child's amazing deeds. Be supportive, not competitive.

Marilee just refused to participate in the Mommy Wars and realized that this was one friendship she would have to give up. Whenever she saw her neighbor's stroller at the park, she would walk on by and come back another time. If she got stuck in a conversation with this woman, she would just change the subject or make an excuse to leave. She refused to let this woman have the power to make her feel inferior as a mother. Marilee recognized that this woman had a need for superiority and was probably very insecure about herself. It wasn't the kind of friendship that Marilee chose to encourage.

FIVE WAYS A BABY WILL ENHANCE AND ENCOURAGE YOUR FRIENDSHIPS

The most beautiful discovery true friends make is that they can grow separately without growing apart.

—Elisabeth Foley

Of course, change isn't always bad. In fact, it can often lead to better things! Maintaining friendships may indeed become more challenging with the arrival of children, but you'll also find more opportunities to make friends as being a parent immerses you in more social situations and gives you common ground to share with other couples.

You'll Meets Tons of People—and Find That Sharing Parenthood Is a Great Foundation for Friendship

If you've ever experienced difficulty making friends because you just couldn't find someone with whom you have much in common, it's about to become easier for you. When you're a parent, a natural bond forms between you and other parents. You and the couple next door may have different lifestyles, careers, tastes, and ways of thinking, but if you both have children at similar ages, you'll never lack topics for conversation. Marilee got a taste of this when Ben was born.

Before having the baby, Marilee hadn't been particularly close with her neighbors. But now that they were running into each other at the park and when she or Brock was pushing the baby in the stroller, they were meeting some great people! She and Brock were really starting to feel part of the community. Having the baby along was always a great icebreaker in starting up conversations with people they met. Most people naturally gravitated toward the baby, asking about him, and before long they were talking about all kinds of things. Marilee and Brock were also making more friends at work and the daycare center now that they had parenthood in common. Being parents opened up a whole new world of friendship for Marilee and Brock.

> *My daycare provider has become my best friend. I know she has my baby's best interests at heart and loves her dearly. I'm so happy to find someone who doesn't mind talking about my daughter's nap schedule and who can help me figure out what's wrong when my daughter's cranky or not well. It's like having a second mom for my daughter.*
>
> —Rebekah Pederson, a new mother

Questions for Discussion

❁ Has your circle of friends expanded to include other parents?

_____

_____

❁ Do you find that your child is often an icebreaker in getting conversations started?

_____

_____

❀ Have you met more of your neighbors now that you're out and about with the baby?

_____

_____

❀ Do you find yourself spending more time now with friends who have children or are expecting?

_____

_____

> ### Take Action!
>
> Sign up for a Mommy & Me, Daddy & Me, or baby massage class—someplace where you will be exposed to more parents of young children. (If you're expecting a baby, join a "taking care of baby" class!) Take the baby for stroller rides around your neighborhood or to the park. You'll be surprised at how many people you'll start meeting!

You'll Get More Breaks and Respect from Other Parents

Parents often get more breaks from other people, especially other parents. Let's say a woman at work leaves the office promptly at five each and every day—announcing that she cannot stay longer, especially for spur-of-the-moment meetings. You may say to yourself, "When she's not at those meetings, it means we have to check with her the next day on certain things, so her not being there means delayed decision making, which makes for more work for the rest of us." But if you know she is the mother of a young child, you may very well cut her more slack because you know she must relieve a sitter and probably has little or no alternative to being away in certain situations.

So there is not only more leeway in terms of how much slack someone will cut the parent of an infant, but also a great deal of respect that comes with the territory of being a new parent. Who doesn't see a parent carrying a young child and immediately say, "Ooh! a new baby"? Who doesn't open the door or let the new parent cut ahead in the line at the grocery store? Why do we do this? For one, we value the workload the new mom or dad has: We know they could use six hands, and we go out of our way to show them support and courtesy. This respect spills over to the workplace. Again, we know our colleague has a great responsibility to deal with, and anyone taking on both work and childcare gets our respect— and maybe even our empathy.

> *I'm very addicted to my daughter. She's two and is so unbelievably darling.*
>
> —Greg Kinnear

People see parenthood as a valued status. Because you're a parent yourself, this makes it easier for you to make friends and influence people—especially at work. And when other parents see you as a fellow authority on raising kids, they're more likely to strike up a conversation with you about your children and parenting, making it easier to cultivate friendships. This is especially true in social situations. Others may not know how to discuss with you the million-dollar stock trade you just made for a big client, but when they learn you're new parent, that's an easy and user-friendly topic; who doesn't want to talk about his or her child?

Marilee and Brock used to avoid going to Brock's company parties or gatherings for the teachers at Marilee's school. It seemed like everyone at these events was talking about their children! They didn't really mind—after all, Marilee became a teacher because she loved children—but they just couldn't contribute to the conversation when everyone started comparing notes on dealing with a picky eater or the best brand of diapers to buy. They almost felt as if others were looking down on them for not having children. Their friends would be talking about buying car seats, and what did Marilee and Brock know about that? They had no knowledge of the subject matter. But when Brock's company announced plans for a summer staff picnic the year after Ben was born, they couldn't wait to go! In fact, since bringing children was encouraged, they could attend with the baby. It seemed to them like they were viewed with new respect. Other parents asked their opinions on parenting issues, and they left the picnic with the phone numbers of several new friends.

Questions for Discussion

✿ Do you feel a new undercurrent of respect from other parents now that you're a parent yourself?

_____

_____

✿ Do you tend to be less judgmental of others or more willing to accommodate them if you know they're parents?

_____

_____

✿ Do you feel more comfortable striking up a conversation with other parents now that you have a child?

_____

_____

Take Action!

Be prepared for that next social situation! Make sure you have a few cute, current pictures of your baby in your purse or wallet. And write down the adorable things your child says or does so you don't forget them. In fact, it's a good idea to do this anyway so that you'll have these memories of the baby years to share with your child. But remember, just as much as you like to talk about your kid, others do too! So make sure not to monopolize the conversation; give others time to chat about their children. It should be a give-and-take, not a one-child show. This is the best way to make—and keep—friends!

You'll Value Friends—They're a Necessary Reprieve from the Demands of Parenting

Although friendships can suffer when you're meeting the demands of new parenthood, it doesn't change these facts: You still need your friends and you will value them more. Your spouse and child can't possibly meet all of your needs. Sometimes you just need an objective friend to hear you out and remind you of who you really are besides your baby's mommy or daddy. A good friend will help you deal with your new stresses and even enable you to get out of the house once in a while, as Marilee found.

> *The best time to make friends is before you need them.*
>
> —Ethel Barrymore

Before Marilee spent the reunion weekend with Cathy, she hadn't realized how stressful the demands of parenthood were. She and Cathy got massages at the hotel and wined and dined themselves. They even got some shopping done without Marilee having to worry about the baby getting impatient! Marilee missed Ben, but she realized that being with Cathy provided a necessary outlet for the stress she had been under. She felt really refreshed and spoiled when she returned home and was ready to tackle the demands of parenthood again with a renewed excitement. It was nice to experience the "real world" with Cathy for a while.

Brock also found that his weekly basketball games were a great outlet for the added stress he was under. The physical exercise coupled with his friends' camaraderie helped him relax and think about something other than the anxieties of supporting a family.

Questions for Discussion

● Do your friends help you escape from the pressures of parenthood?

_____

_____

● Do you call a friend when you're feeling stressed out from taking care of a baby?

_____

_____

● What things do you like to do with your friends that you can't do with a baby along?

_____

_____

🌸 Do you make an effort to continue spending time alone with friends?

_____
_____

> ### Take Action!
> The next time you're feeling stressed, pick up the phone and call a good friend. Make arrangements for an outing without the children. Line up childcare and just resolve to have fun! Think about something you've been longing to do but have put off because you can't take the baby along. It might be seeing a movie or play, getting a haircut or manicure, going to the spa, or shopping. Just having this event to look forward to will help alleviate the stress!

You Will Benefit from the Experience and Advice Friends Give

You're going to have questions when you're a new parent—lots of them! Don't be afraid to ask for help. Seasoned parents are great resources for in-the-trenches advice. Which style of pacifier do babies like best? Are generic diapers as good as brand name? How can I get my baby to eat her cereal? Ask a parent. You'll appreciate your friends who are parents more than ever.

Marilee picked up lots of great parenting tips from other mothers at work. She found her daycare center when it came highly recommended by the third-grade teacher. And when her baby was having trouble tolerating a particular formula, a suggestion from a coworker was just the ticket! Being around other mothers was like having her own personal motherhood guide. One friend told her about a great stroller-accessible park that she had never even realized existed, although it was just a few miles from her house.

In fact, whenever Marilee and Brock had a question about parenting, they polled their own personal panel of experts at work or in their neighborhood and, more often than not, ended up with the answer they needed. It was wonderful having this connection with their coworkers and neighbors, and they forged many new friendships in this manner.

Questions for Discussion

❀ Who do you go to for parenting advice (besides your doctor)?

_____

_____

❀ Is it helpful to get other parents' opinions before making parenting decisions?

_____

_____

❀ What tips have you picked up from other parents?

_____

_____

❀ How does sharing parenthood experiences aid in developing friendships?

_____

_____

People love to offer their opinions. The next time you're puzzled about where to have your child's birthday party or which stroller is most durable, ask another parent, or two or more. Oftentimes, you'll find a pattern emerging that will lead you to the best answers. Don't be shy about soliciting advice (or feel you necessarily have to take it). Build a community of "wise parents" whose experience can get you through your first year.

Some Friends Will Become a Wonderful
Part of Your Child's Life

You may assume that your friends who are parents will be the biggest help with your children, but you may be surprised to find that even friends without young children can become part of your parenting team. Older people whose own kids are grown might love to hold a new baby in their arms again, and often have plenty of time and patience to spend with a needy child. It's always helpful to have a few surrogate grandmas who would jump at the chance to tend to your baby while you get a needed break for lunch. And younger adults who haven't yet had children may find that they love getting their "baby fix" by looking after your child in preparation for having their own someday. Marilee and Brock were pleased to find their own aunt-in-the-making when Ben was born.

Marilee and Brock's older neighbor Agnes became almost a second mom to the baby. She lived on her own and her grown children lived far away, so she really doted on baby Ben and often bought him small gifts or offered to take him around the block in the stroller. Although Marilee and Agnes didn't appear on the surface to have a lot in common, their shared love for the baby brought them closer together and forged a friendship between them. Ben loved his "Aunt Aggie," and the relationship was good for Agnes as well, because she so looked forward to her times with the baby.

> *I love children, especially when they cry, because then somebody takes them away.*
>
> —Nancy Mitford

Questions for Discussion

❀ Do you have a single or childless friend who has become an honorary aunt or uncle to your child?

_____

_____

❀ How does this relationship benefit your child? How does it benefit your friend?

_____

_____

❀ Has your shared love for your child brought you closer to this friend?

_____

_____

> **Take Action!**
>
> If you don't have a lot of extended family around, don't hesitate to appoint an eager honorary aunt or uncle to fulfill this position. It's a win-win situation for everyone. The baby loves the extra attention. Your friend loves spending time with your child. And you'll get closer to your friend as well as have an available babysitter or someone to hang out with. There are all kinds of ways to build a family for your child.

CONCLUSION

Friends come; friends go. Friendships evolve. Early parenthood is a time when you'll see a lot of this going on! But it's the natural scheme of life. Cherish your "pre-baby" friendships and do all you can to preserve them, but also recognize that some will fall by the wayside—and that's normal, too. Understand that your relationships may go through an adaptation phase as you adjust to the addition of a baby in your lives. And nurture your new friendships, as friends are very important when you're a new parent. Of course you're busy, but make as much of an effort as possible to maintain your friendships. Whether you are home with a little baby or juggling career and parenthood, the first year can be a lonely and uncertain time. Welcome the help and joy that others bring into your life. Make friends . . . and be a friend!

> *I always say that I think God didn't let me have kids so all kids in the world could be mine. . . ..*
>
> —Dolly Parton

About the Authors

Bettie B. Youngs, Ed.D., Ph.D., is the award-winning author of thirty-two books translated into twenty-seven languages. Dr. Youngs is a former Teacher-of-the-Year, University Professor of Graduate School education, and Director of Instruction and Professional Development, Inc. Bettie has frequently appeared on *The Good Morning Show*, *NBC Nightly News*, *CNN*, and *Oprah*. *USA Today*, the *Washington Post*, *Time Magazine*, *Redbook*, *McCall's*, *U.S. News & World Report*, *Working Woman*, *Family Circle*, *Parents Magazine*, and *PTA* have all recognized her work. Dr. Youngs is the author of a number of videocassette programs and is the coauthor of the nationally acclaimed *Parents on Board*, a video-based training program to help schools and parents work together to increase student well-being and achievement. Bettie serves on the Boards of a number of organizations and is the recipient of numerous service awards for her contribution to community activities. She works with parents and schools nationwide. Bettie is the mother of Jennifer L. Youngs, and grandmother to Kendahl Brooke Youngs!

Susan M. Heim is a writer and editor, specializing in parenting, women's, and Christian issues. She enjoys developing book ideas and editing books with many high-profile authors. Before starting her own writing and editing business, Susan was a Senior Editor at Health Communications, Inc., where she was a lead editor for the bestselling *Chicken Soup for the Soul series*, as well as all religion and teen books. Her books include, *Twice the Love: Stories of Inspiration for the Parents of Twins and Multiples*, published in conjunction with Twins magazine,. Susan has a degree in Business Administration from Michigan

State University. She lives in Boca Raton, Florida, with her husband Mike and their four sons.

Jennifer Leigh Youngs is the author of *Moments and Milestones Pregnancy Journal: A Week-by-Week Companion; Feeling Great, Looking Hot and Loving Yourself: Health, Fitness and Beauty for Teens; Confidence & Self-Esteem for Teens; Health & Fitness for Teens; Problem Solving Skills for Children 5-12* and coauthor of the popular *Taste Berries for Teens* series (ten self-help books for ages 10–18). Jennifer is a former Miss Teen California finalist and a Rotary International Goodwill Ambassador and Exchange Scholar. She is a volunteer with Airline Ambassadors, an international organization affiliated with the United Nations that aims to develop cross-cultural friendships by escorting children to hospitals for medical care and orphans to new homes throughout the world, and delivers humanitarian aid to orphanages and those in need worldwide. She lives in Southern California with her husband Rick, and daughter Kendahl Brooke Youngs.

Other Books by Bettie Youngs Book Publishers

Healthy Family, Happy Life
What Healthy Families Learn from Healthy Moms

Donna Schuller

Family, Health, Fitness & Nutrition expert Donna Schuller offers advice for improving health and wellness including the benefits the and paybacks of being honest with others; how wellness thoughts contribute to your being healthy; the significance of loving others and the imperative of loving oneself of exercise, sleep and happiness; how to get through hard times; how dietary supplementation work; the importance of nutrition, and more.

ISBN: 978-1-940784-11-3 • ePub: 978-1-940784-31-1

Confidence & Self-Esteem for Teens

Jennifer L. Youngs

Confidence & Self-Esteem for Teens is about the ways that beauty manifests from within. Have you ever run across someone who looked pretty, but undid her beauty by the way she acted or treated others?

Compare that to someone who is thoughtful, confident and comfortable with herself and as a result, has a lovely presence about her.

This book shows you how to let your inner beauty shine through—things like the secrets of serenity, steps for staying cool under pressure, building your self-esteem, drawing security from loving others, setting goals and feeling purposeful—and more.

ISBN: 978-1-940784-35-9 • ePub: 978-1-940784-34-2

Health & Fitness for Teens

Jennifer L. Youngs

Health & Fitness for Teens covers a most essential topic for teens: having a healthy body, liking your body and being fit. It's also a time of constant change. We can feel like we're just getting to know who we are when suddenly we are someone totally different. This book uncovers some of the myths teens have for comparing themselves to a standard other than their own, and covers some very important ground on how to best take care of themselves so as to look and feel their very best.

ISBN: 978-1-940784-33-5• ePub: 978-1-940784-32-8

179

Problem Solving Skills for Children Ages 5-12

Jennifer L. Youngs

This skill book for children, ages 5-12, teaches a 5-step process to help children learn a simple process to solve problems. Ideal for parents, educators and home-schooled courses to use with children. Written for the child him/herself, children are taught given ample practice by helping others solve their problems.

ISBN: 978-1-940784-11-3 • Epub: 978-1-940784-31-1

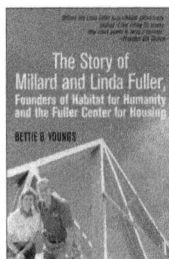

The Story of Millard and Linda Fuller, Founders of Habitat for Humanity and The Fuller Center for Housing

Bettie B. Youngs

Everyone has heard of Habitat for Humanity, the faith-based housing initiative that has built homes for more than a million of the world's poor. Many are familiar with its founders, Millard and Linda Fuller. But few know the amazing love story behind the movement—a story that began accidentally and will conclude in a world forever changed by its impact.

By age 29, Millard Fuller was a self-made millionaire. But that success came at a cost. He never took a family vacation, had kids he barely knew, and a lonely wife who was about to leave him. Ultimately, realizing that he was about to lose what really mattered, Fuller reconciled with his wife and rearranged his priorities.

In 1965, the Fullers gave away their personal fortune and dedicated their lives to serving others, eventually founding Habitat for Humanity in 1976. In this capacity, the Fullers traveled the globe, receiving the praise of prime ministers and presidents, sharing meals with prisoners, and appealing for funds and volunteers. More important than any accolade or award were the homes they built and the hope they gave. The Fullers have done more for the cause of housing the poor than any other couple in history.

Eventually, a struggle for the reins of the most beloved nonprofit of our times would result in the firing of Millard and Linda by Habitat International's board of directors. This certainly didn't mean the end of their vision—the Fullers would rebound, continuing to support local Habitat affiliates and beginning The Fuller Center for Housing, determined to pursue their dream of building for people everywhere simple, decent places to live.

ISBN: 978-0-9882848-8-3 • Epub: 978-1-936332-53-3

Hostage of Paradox: *A Qualmish Disclosure*

John Rixey Moore

Few people then or now know about the clandestine war that the CIA ran in Vietnam, using the Green Berets for secret operations throughout Southeast Asia. This was not the Vietnam War of the newsreels, the body counts, rice paddy footage, and men smoking cigarettes on the sandbag bunkers. This was a shadow directive of deep-penetration interdiction, reconnaissance, and assassination missions conducted by a selected few Special Forces units, deployed quietly from forward operations bases to prowl through agendas that, for security reasons, were seldom understood by the men themselves.

Hostage of Paradox is the first-hand account by one of these elite team leaders.

"Deserving of a place in the upper ranks of Vietnam War memoirs." —**Kirkus Review**

"Read this book, you'll be, as John Moore puts it, 'transfixed, like kittens in a box.'" —**David Willson, Book Review, The VVA Veteran**

ISBN: 978-1-936332-37-3 • ePub: 978-1-936332-33-5

The Maybelline Story
And the Spirited Family Dynasty Behind It

Sharrie Williams

A fascinating and inspiring story, a tale both epic and intimate, alive with the clash, the hustle, the music, and dance of American enterprise.

"A richly told story of a forty-year, white-hot love triangle that fans the flames of a major worldwide conglomerate." —**Neil Shulman, Associate Producer,** *Doc Hollywood*

"Salacious! Engrossing! There are certain stories so dramatic, so sordid, that they seem positively destined for film; this is one of them." —*New York Post*

ISBN: 978-0-9843081-1-8 • ePub: 978-1-936332-17-5

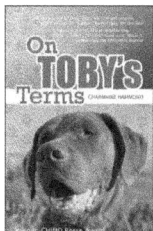

On Toby's Terms

Charmaine Hammond

On Toby's Terms is an endearing story of a beguiling creature who teaches his owners that, despite their trying to teach him how to be the dog they want, he is the one to lay out the terms of being the dog he needs to be. This insight would change their lives forever.

"This is a captivating, heartwarming story and we are very excited about bringing it to film." —**Steve Hudis, Producer**

ISBN: 978-0-9843081-4-9 • ePub: 978-1-936332-15-1

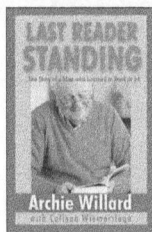

Last Reader Standing
... The Story of a Man Who Learned to Read at 54

Archie Willard
with Colleen Wiemerslage

The day Archie lost his thirty-one year job as a laborer at a meat packing company, he was forced to confront the secret he had held so closely for most of his life: at the age of fifty-four, he couldn't read. For all his adult life, he'd been able to skirt around the issue. But now, forced to find a new job to support his family, he could no longer hide from the truth.

Last Reader Standing is the story of Archie's amazing—and often painful—journey of becoming literate at middle age, struggling with the newfound knowledge of his dyslexia. From the little boy who was banished to the back of the classroom because the teachers labeled him "stupid," Archie emerged to becoming a national figure who continues to enlighten professionals into the world of the learning disabled. He joined Barbara Bush on stage for her Literacy Foundation's fundraisers where she proudly introduced him as "the man who took advantage of a second chance and improved his life."

This is a touching and poignant story that gives us an eye-opening view of the lack of literacy in our society, and how important it is for all of us to have opportunity to become all that we can be—to have hope and go after our dreams.

At the age of eighty-two, Archie continues to work with literacy issues in medicine and consumerism.

"Archie . . . you need to continue spreading the word." **—Barbara Bush, founder of the Literacy Foundation, and First Lady and wife of George H. W. Bush, the 41st President of the United States**

ISBN: 978-1-936332-48-9 • ePub: 978-1-936332-50-2

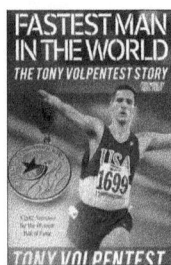

Fastest Man in the World
The Tony Volpentest Story

Tony Volpentest
Foreword by Ross Perot

Tony Volpentest, a four-time Paralympic gold medalist and five-time world champion sprinter, is a 2012 nominee for the Olympic Hall of Fame. This inspirational story details his being born without feet, to holding records as the fastest sprinter in the world.

"This inspiring story is about the thrill of victory to be sure—winning gold—but it is also a reminder about human potential: the willingness to push ourselves beyond the ledge of our own imagination. A powerfully inspirational story." **—Charlie Huebner, United States Olympic Committee**

ISBN: 978-1-940784-07-6 • ePub: 978-1-940784-08-3

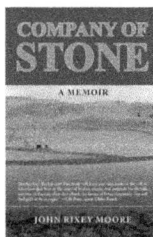

Company of Stone

John Rixey Moore

With yet unhealed wounds from recent combat, John Moore undertook an unexpected walking tour in the rugged Scottish highlands. With the approach of a season of freezing rainstorms he took shelter in a remote monastery—a chance encounter that would change his future, his beliefs about blind chance, and the unexpected courses by which the best in human nature can smuggle its way into the life of a stranger. Afterwards, a chance conversation overheard in a village pub steered him to Canada, where he took a job as a rock drill operator in a large industrial gold mine. The dangers he encountered among the lost men in that dangerous other world, secretive men who sought permanent anonymity in the perils of work deep underground—a brutal kind of monasticism itself—challenged both his endurance and his sense of humanity.

With sensitivity and delightful good humor, Moore explores the surprising lessons learned in these strangely rich fraternities of forgotten men—a brotherhood housed in crumbling medieval masonry, and one shared in the unforgiving depths of the gold mine.

ISBN: 978-1-936332-44-1 • ePub: 978-1-936332-45-8

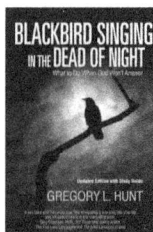

Blackbird Singing in the Dead of Night
What to Do When God Won't Answer

Updated Edition with Study Guide

Gregory L. Hunt

Pastor Greg Hunt had devoted nearly thirty years to congregational ministry, helping people experience God and find their way in life. Then came his own crisis of faith and calling. While turning to God for guidance, he finds nothing. Neither his education nor his religious involvements could prepare him for the disorienting impact of the experience. Alarmed, he tries an experiment. The result is startling—and changes his life entirely.

"Compelling. If you have ever longed to hear God whispering a love song into your life, read this book." —**Gary Chapman**, *NY Times* **bestselling author,** *The Love Languages of God*

ISBN: 978-0-9882848-9-0 • ePub: 978-1-936332-52-6

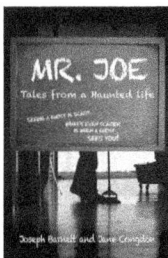

MR. JOE
Tales from a Haunted Life

Joseph Barnett and Jane Congdon

Do you believe in ghosts? Joseph Barnett didn't, until the winter he was fired from his career job and became a school custodian. Assigned the graveyard shift, Joe was confronted with a series of bizarre and terrifying occurrences.

"Thrilling, thoughtful, elegantly told. So much more than a ghost story."
—**Cyrus Webb, CEO, Conversation Book Club**

ISBN: 978-1-936332-78-6 • ePub: 978-1-936332-79-3

183

The Rebirth of Suzzan Blac

Suzzan Blac

A horrific upbringing and then abduction into the sex slave industry would all but kill Suzzan's spirit to live. But a happy marriage and two children brought love—and forty-two stunning paintings, art so raw that it initially frightened even the artist. "I hid the pieces for 15 years," says Suzzan, "but just as with the secrets in this book, I am slowing sneaking them out, one by one by one." Now a renowned artist, her work is exhibited world-wide. A story of inspiration, truth and victory.

"A solid memoir about a life reconstructed. Chilling, thrilling, and thought provoking."
—Pearry Teo, Producer, *The Gene Generation*

ISBN: 978-1-936332-22-9 • ePub: 978-1-936332-23-6

Voodoo in My Blood
A Healer's Journey from Surgeon to Shaman

Carolle Jean-Murat, M.D.

Born and raised in Haiti to a family of healers, US trained physician Carolle Jean-Murat came to be regarded as a world-class surgeon. But her success harbored a secret: in the operating room, she could quickly intuit the root cause of her patient's illness, often times knowing she could help the patient without surgery. Carolle knew that to fellow surgeons, her intuition was best left unmentioned. But when the devastating earthquake hit Haiti and Carolle returned to help, she had to acknowledge the shaman she had become.

"This fascinating memoir sheds light on the importance of asking yourself, 'Have I created for myself the life I've meant to live?'" **—Christiane Northrup, M.D., author of the New York Times bestsellers:** *Women's Bodies, Women's Wisdom*

ISBN: 978-1-936332-05-2 • ePub: 978-1-936332-04-5

Electric Living
The Science behind the Law of Attraction

Kolie Crutcher

An electrical engineer by training, Crutcher applies his in-depth knowledge of electrical engineering principles and practical engineering experience detailing the scientific explanation of why human beings become what they think. A practical, step-by-step guide to help you harness your thoughts and emotions so that the Law of Attraction will benefit you.

ISBN: 978-1-936332-58-8 • ePub: 978-1-936332-59-5

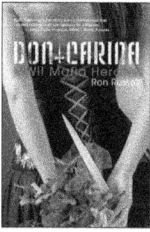

DON CARINA: WWII Mafia Heroine

Ron Russell

A father's death in Southern Italy in the 1930s—a place where women who can read are considered unfit for marriage—thrusts seventeen-year-old Carina into servitude as a "black widow," a legal head of the household who cares for her twelve siblings. A scandal forces her into a marriage to Russo, the "Prince of Naples." By cunning force, Carina seizes control of Russo's organization and disguising herself as a man, controls the most powerful of Mafia groups for nearly a decade.

"A woman as the head of the Mafia who shows her family her resourcefulness, strength and survival techniques. Unique, creative and powerful! This exciting book blends history, intrigue and power into one delicious epic adventure that you will not want to put down!" —**Linda Gray, Actress,** *Dallas*

ISBN: 978-0-9843081-9-4 • ePub: 978-1-936332-49-6

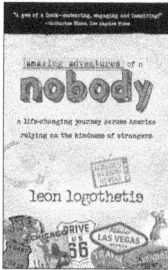

Amazing Adventures of a Nobody

Leon Logothetis

From the Hit Television Series Aired in 100 Countries!

Tired of his disconnected life and uninspiring job, Leon Logothetis leaves it all behind—job, money, home, even his cell phone—and hits the road with nothing but the clothes on his back and five dollars in his pocket, relying on the kindness of strangers and the serendipity of the open road for his daily keep. Masterful story-telling!

"A gem of a book; endearing, engaging and inspiring." —**Catharine Hamm, Los Angeles Times Travel Editor**

ISBN: 978-0-9843081-3-2 • ePub: 978-1-936332-51-9

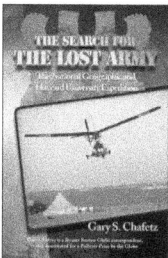

The Search for the Lost Army
The National Geographic and Harvard University Expedition

Gary S. Chafetz

In one of history's greatest ancient disasters, a Persian army of 50,000 soldiers was suffocated by a hurricane-force sandstorm in 525 BC in Egypt's Western Desert. No trace of this conquering army, hauling huge quantities of looted gold and silver, has ever surfaced.

Gary Chafetz, referred to as "one of the ten best journalists of the past twenty-five years," is a former Boston Globe correspondent and was twice nominated for a Pulitzer Prize by the Globe.

ISBN: 978-1-936332-98-4 • ePub: 978-1-936332-99-1

185

Out of the Transylvania Night

Aura Imbarus
A Pulitzer-Prize entry

"I'd grown up in the land of Transylvania, homeland to Dracula, Vlad the Impaler, and worse, dictator Nicolae Ceausescu," writes the author. "Under his rule, like vampires, we came to life after sundown, hiding our heirloom jewels and documents deep in the earth." Fleeing to the US to rebuild her life, she discovers a startling truth about straddling two cultures and striking a balance between one's dreams and the sacrifices that allow a sense of "home."

"Aura's courage shows the degree to which we are all willing to live lives centered on freedom, hope, and an authentic sense of self. Truly a love story!" —**Nadia Comaneci, Olympic Champion**

ISBN: 978-0-9843081-2-5 • ePub: 978-1-936332-20-5

Living with Multiple Personalities
The Christine Ducommun Story

Christine Ducommun

Christine Ducommun was a happily married wife and mother of two, when— after moving back into her childhood home—she began to experience panic attacks and bizarre flashbacks. Eventually diagnosed with Dissociative Identity Disorder (DID), Christine's story details an extraordinary twelve-year ordeal unraveling the buried trauma of her forgotten past.

"Reminiscent of the Academy Award-winning *A Beautiful Mind*, this true story will have you on the edge of your seat. Spellbinding!" —**Josh Miller, Producer**

ISBN: 978-0-9843081-5-6 • ePub: 978-1-936332-06-9

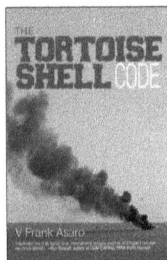

The Tortoise Shell Code

V Frank Asaro

Off the coast of Southern California, the Sea Diva, a tuna boat, sinks. Members of the crew are missing and what happened remains a mystery. Anthony Darren, a renowned and wealthy lawyer at the top of his game, knows the boat's owner and soon becomes involved in the case. As the case goes to trial, a missing crew member is believed to be at fault, but new evidence comes to light and the finger of guilt points in a completely unanticipated direction. An action-packed thriller.

ISBN: 978-1-936332-60-1 • ePub: 978-1-936332-61-8

186

A World Torn Asunder
The Life and Triumph of Constantin C. Giurescu

Marina Giurescu, M.D.

Constantin C. Giurescu was Romania's leading historian and author. His granddaughter's fascinating story of this remarkable man and his family follows their struggles in war-torn Romania from 1900 to the fall of the Soviet Union. An "enlightened" society is dismantled with the 1946 Communist takeover of Romania, and Constantin is confined to the notorious Sighet penitentiary. Drawing on her grandfather's prison diary (which was put in a glass jar, buried in a yard, then smuggled out of the country by Dr. Paul E. Michelson—who does the FOREWORD for this book), private letters and her own research, Dr. Giurescu writes of the legacy from the turn of the century to the fall of Communism.

We see the rise of modern Romania, the misery of World War I, the blossoming of its culture between the wars, and then the sellout of Eastern Europe to Russia after World War II. In this sweeping account, we see not only its effects socially and culturally, but the triumph in its wake: a man and his people who reclaim better lives for themselves, and in the process, teach us a lesson in endurance, patience, and will—not only to survive, but to thrive.

"The inspirational story of a quiet man and his silent defiance in the face of tyranny."
—**Dr. Connie Mariano, author of** *The White House Doctor*

ISBN: 978-1-936332-76-2 • ePub: 978-1-936332-77-9

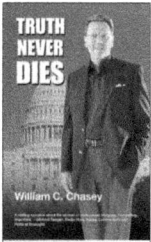

Truth Never Dies
William C. Chasey

A lobbyist for some 40 years, William C. Chasey represented some of the world's most prestigious business clients and twenty-three foreign governments before the US Congress. His integrity never questioned. All that changed when Chasey was hired to forge communications between Libya and the US Congress. A trip he took with a US Congressman for discussions with then Libyan leader Muammar Qadhafi forever changed Chasey's life. Upon his return, his bank accounts were frozen, clients and friends had been advised not to take his calls.

Things got worse: the CIA, FBI, IRS, and the Federal Judiciary attempted to coerce him into using his unique Libyan access to participate in a CIA-sponsored assassination plot of the two Libyans indicted for the bombing of Pan Am flight 103. Chasey's refusal to cooperate resulted in a six-year FBI investigation and sting operation, financial ruin, criminal charges, and incarceration in federal prison.

"A chilling narrative about the abuses of state power. Intriguing! Compelling. Important."
—**Michael Reagan, Radio Host, Author, Commentator and Political Strategist**

"An unprecedented first hand look into the chilling world of Libyan Leader Muammar Qadhafi by the man who risked it all to resolve the dispute between the United States and Libya over the Lockerbie bombing. This is sure to be an unforgettable motion picture."
—**Peter Tomaszewicz, Producer, Truth Never Dies**

ISBN: 978-1-936332-46-5 • ePub: 978-1-936332-47-2

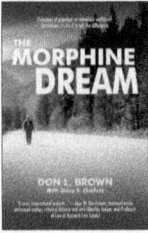

The Morphine Dream

Don Brown with *Pulitzer nominated Gary S. Chafetz*

At 36, high-school dropout and a failed semi-professional ballplayer Donald Brown hit bottom when an industrial accident left him immobilized. But Brown had a dream while on a morphine drip after surgery: he imagined himself graduating from Harvard Law School (he was a classmate of Barack Obama) and walking across America. Brown realizes both seemingly unreachable goals, and achieves national recognition as a legal crusader for minority homeowners. An intriguing tale of his long walk—both physical and metaphorical. A story of perseverance and second chances. Sheer inspiration for those wishing to reboot their lives.

"An incredibly inspirational memoir." —**Alan M. Dershowitz, professor, Harvard Law School**

ISBN: 978-1-936332-25-0 • ePub: 978-1-936332-39-7

The Girl Who Gave Her Wish Away

Sharon Babineau
Foreword by Craig Kielburger

The Children's Wish Foundation approached lovely thirteen-year-old Maddison Babineau just after she received her cancer diagnosis. "You can have anything," they told her, "a Disney cruise? The chance to meet your favorite movie star? A five thousand dollar shopping spree?"

Maddie knew exactly what she wanted. She had recently been moved to tears after watching a television program about the plight of orphaned children. Maddie's wish? To ease the suffering of these children half-way across the world. Despite the ravishing cancer, she became an indefatigable fundraiser for "her children." In The Girl Who Gave Wish Away, her mother reveals Maddie's remarkable journey of providing hope and future to the village children who had filled her heart.

A special story, heartwarming and reassuring.

ISBN: 978-1-936332-96-0 • ePub: 978-1-936332-97-7

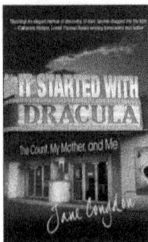

It Started with Dracula
The Count, My Mother, and Me

Jane Congdon

The terrifying legend of Count Dracula silently skulking through the Transylvania night may have terrified generations of filmgoers, but the tall, elegant vampire captivated and electrified a young Jane Congdon, igniting a dream to one day see his mysterious land of ancient castles and misty hollows. Four decades later she finally takes her long-awaited trip—never dreaming that it would unearth decades-buried memories, and trigger a life-changing inner journey. A memoir full of surprises, Jane's story is one of hope, love—and second chances.

ISBN: 978-1-936332-10-6 • ePub: 978-1-936332-11-3

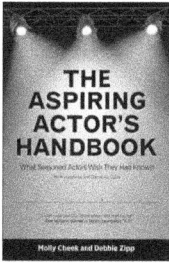

The Aspiring Actor's Handbook

Molly Cheek and Debbie Zip

Concise and straightforward, The Aspiring Actor's Handbook is written for curious and aspiring actors to help them make informed decisions while pursuing this exciting career.

Veteran actresses Molly Cheek and Debbie Zipp have culled the wit and wisdom of a wide array of successful actors, from Beth Grant to Dee Wallace, and collected the kind of mentoring perspective so many in the business wish they'd had when they were just starting out. Get insider information and real-life experiences and personal stories that range from how to get your foot in the door to becoming a career actor. Get the inside scoop from successful veteran actors on how to work with agents and unions; manage finances; prepare for auditions; cope with rejection—and success—and much more.

ISBN: 978-1-940784-12-0 • ePub: 978-1-940784-02-1

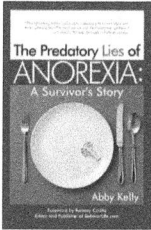

The Predatory Lies of Anorexia
A Survivor's Story

Abby D. Kelly

"I want...I want you to think I am the smartest, the thinnest, the most beautiful..."

With these words, Abby Kelly encapsulates the overwhelming struggle of her 15-year bout with anorexia. Abby lays bare the reality of anorexia, beginning in her teenage years, when the predatory lies of the disease took root in her psyche as she felt pressured from family and peers for not being "enough." In her quest for a greater sense of personal power, she concludes "I'll be 'more', but it will be on my terms."

Her reasoning is a classic example as to why and how eating disorders dig in and persist as long as they do.

From this new self-awareness, Abby targets her body as the agent to show others that she is disciplined and focused. She sets out to restrict her food intake and adheres to an extreme schedule of exercise. While others close to Abby see a person who is dangerously thin, Abby, in fact, derives a sense of personal achievement from her weight loss.

Abby exposes the battles, defeats, and ultimate triumph—taking the reader on a poignant odyssey from onset to recovery, including how she set out to fool the many who tried to help her, from dietitians to therapists, from one inpatient treatment center after another, and reveals not only the victim's suffering, but that of those who love her.

This raw and passionate story eloquently describes how Abby finally freed herself from this life-threatening condition, and how others can find courage and hope for recovery, too.

"This beautifully written book paints an exacting picture of Anorexia, one that is sure to help legions of those suffering from this most serious and life-threatening condition."
—Amy Dardis, founder and editor of Haven Journal

ISBN: 978-1-940784-17-5 • ePub: 978-1-940784-18-2

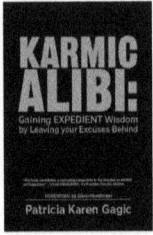

Karmic Alibi

Gaining EXPEDIENT Wisdom by Leaving Your Excuses Behind

Patricia Karen Gagic

Karma is a potent law of the universe. Karma, literally meaning "action," is the sum of your intentional and deliberate consciousness, which prescribes your thoughts and thus determines your actions.

Just as positive thoughts initiate positive outcomes, negative thoughts create angst. The "wisdom" of your Karma is yours alone; you cannot experience someone else's Karma.

In Karmic Alibi, expert Patricia Gagic shares how you can influence the sovereignty of your Karma. By mastering the "five radical degrees of life" you can expedite the wisdom of your Karma so as to live in a state of joyful and purpose-filled abundance emotionally, physically and spiritually—which is your divine right.

In this soulful and most insightful book, Patricia examines her own beliefs and describes how she transformed them. By using examples from her life, and thanks to the trail markers she leaves along the way, she makes it easier for each of us to create the life we wish to live, too.

ISBN: 978-1-940784-29-8 • ePub: 978-1-940784-30-4

News Girls Don't Cry

Melissa McCarty

Today the host of ORA TV's Newsbreaker, and now calling Larry King her boss, Melissa McCarty worked her way up through the trenches of live television news. But she was also running away from her past, one of growing up in the roughest of neighborhoods, watching so many she knew—including her brother—succumb to drugs, gangs, and violence. It was a past that forced her to be tough and streetwise, traits that in her career as a popular television newscaster, would end up working against her.

Every tragic story she covered was a grim reminder of where she'd been. But the practiced and restrained emotion given to the camera became her protective armor even in her private life where she was unable to let her guard down—a demeanor that damaged both her personal and professional relationships. In News Girls Don't Cry, McCarty confronts the memory-demons of her past, exploring how they hardened her—and how she turned it all around.

An inspiring story of overcoming adversity, welcoming second chances, and becoming happy and authentic.

"A battle between personal success and private anguish, a captivating brave tale of a woman's drive to succed and her tireless struggle to keep her family intact. The reader is pulled into Melissa's story… an honest account of the common battle of addiction." —**Susan Hendricks, CNN Headline News Anchor**

ISBN: 978-1-936332-69-4 • ePub: 978-1-936332-70-0

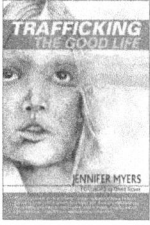

Trafficking the Good Life

Jennifer Myers

Jennifer Myers had worked hard toward a successful career as a dancer in Chicago. But just as her star was rising, she fell for the kingpin of a drug trafficking operation. Drawn to his life of excitement, she soon acquiesced to driving marijuana across the country, making easy money she stacked in shoeboxes and spent like an heiress. Only time in a federal prison made her face up to and understand her choices. It was there, at rock bottom, that she discovered that her real prison was the one she had unwittingly made inside herself and where she could start rebuilding a life of purpose and ethical pursuit.

"In her gripping memoir Jennifer Myers offers a startling account of how the pursuit of an elusive American Dream can lead us to the depths of the American criminal underbelly. Her book is as much about being human in a hyper-materialistic society as it is about drug culture. When the DEA finally knocks on Myers' door, she and the reader both see the moment for what it truly is—not so much an arrest as a rescue." —**Tony D'Souza, author of Whiteman and Mule**

ISBN: 978-1-936332-67-0 • ePub: 978-1-936332-68-7

191

Bettie Youngs Book Publishers and Burres Books

If you are unable to order this book from your local bookseller, or online from Amazon or Barnes & Noble, or from Espresso, or, Read How You Want, or wholesaler Baker & Taylor, you may order directly from the publisher at Sales@BettieYoungsBooks.com.

VISIT OUR WEBSITE AT:
www.BettieYoungsBooks.com

www.ingramcontent.com/pod-product-compliance
Lightning Source LLC
Chambersburg PA
CBHW022019090426

42739CB00006BA/205